"GET OFF MY PITCH"

"GET OFF MY PITCH"

by

Don Gallacher

with
Colin Gallacher

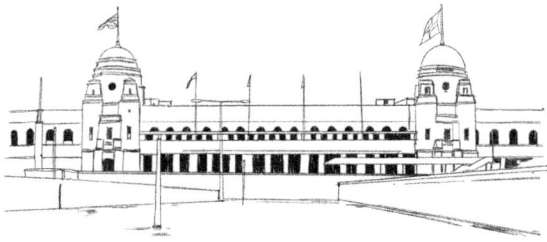

Dedicated to

Donald Frederick Gallacher.

Well, we got there eventually Dad,
sorry it took so long, only you and I know why,
but at last, your Wembley story is being told, I hope you approve.

Colin Gallacher

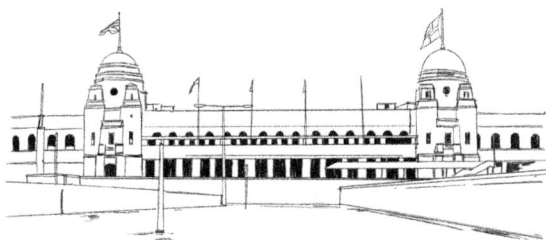

Contents

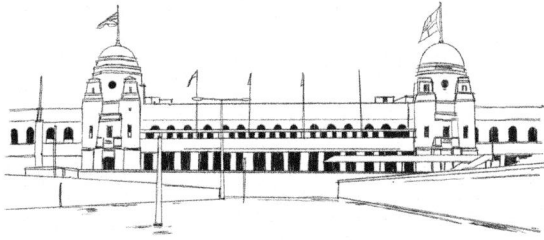

Introduction

The Empire Stadium Wembley
(that's the 'old' one with Twin Towers)

This is a story about a man who spent a large part of his life as Head Groundsman of the 'Old Wembley Stadium'. The one with the Twin Towers, steeped in history and in its heyday, regarded as among the most famous sporting venues in the world.

My father, Don Gallacher had been a groundsman on sports-grounds for most of his life and from modest beginnings, had reached his ultimate goal in 1974 by taking over responsibility for the sacred turf of Wembley and did so for a decade. During which time he made major changes to the playing surface in particular and whilst even now we tend to associate Wembley Stadium (new or old) with a cup final or international football. One rarely considers, that at times, events altered twice weekly - from Football to Rugby, Hockey, Speedway, Greyhound Racing, Rock Concerts, Military Pageants etc. and although the pitch wasn't used as frequently as a typical football league ground, a league ground didn't need to have the lines completely re-marked, the pitch covered in boarding for holding concerts, have the corners dug up to accommodate a speedway track, and still have to live up to its reputation of being the best playing surface and from a purely aesthetic point of view, the best *looking* pitch in the world.

This memoir was written by Don during the decade or so when he was the Head Groundsman and for a period following his enforced retirement when he acted as consultant to his successor at the Empire Stadium.

By recording his experience, he hoped that it would provide a 'pitch eye view' of the original Wembley Stadium that will invoke mainly warm memories for many readers. Not just to the thousands of players that played, or the millions of fans that cheered, but the hundreds of thousands of 'others' from all over the world, who visited the stadium by taking tours when there were no events taking place at all.

This is not a book about soccer, rugby matches or pop concerts although these are of course benchmarks along the way. Equally, whilst the book describes how the turf was created, nurtured, maintained and repaired against adversity, (weather, wear and tear, marching boots or, bureaucracy). Neither is it about turf management. It is about the experiences of the man in the middle of the pitch endeavouring to deliver the highest standards in his 'field' to the finest people in their sport or skill, performing to a worldwide audience, just as his counterparts still do everywhere. There were of course many occasions when his skills and patience were stretched to the limit, such as the England v Scotland International football match in June 1977 when the Scottish fans invaded the pitch tearing down the goals and ripping up the turf, that sent images of Don in the midst of the debacle to TV screens and newspapers all around the world. Which is when I first saw images of my dad on the TV and on the front pages of Sunday newspapers, looking to be, in none-too-pleased mode as shown on the cover photo which became the inspiration for this book.

Colin Gallacher

Son and Grandson of groundsmen

©Photo credit of Mirrorpix/Reach Licensing.

England v Scotland Football International Wembley Stadium 4 June 1977 Scottish fans invade and partially destroy the pitch.

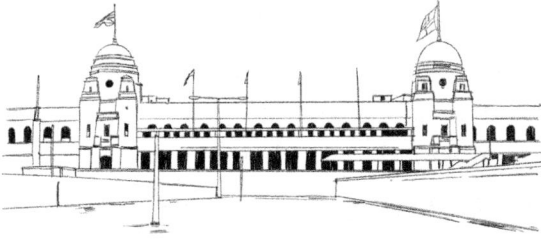

The Turf is Sacred

*T*here is a family story which describes how when I was very small, playing with my brothers on the edge of my dad's sports ground in Tottenham. I tripped and fell on a scythe that some fool had left in the long grass of the outfield. A scythe is a long, curved blade on a long handle used for slicing down long grass. It laid open my young shin almost to the bone and there was blood and gore and much bawling from everywhere. Most of which was naturally coming from me, but not all. My eldest brother Jack took command of the situation snatched me up, threw me into a rickety pushchair that we'd been playing with and set off as fast as he could run in a dead straight line for our house on the far side of the ground. Unfortunately for Jack this 'shortest distance between two points' took him, his patient and pushchair, not to mention a motley band of friends, right across the middle of the precious cricket table. Even more unfortunate, was that our father, the groundsman, had just walked onto the ground returning from his lunch, just in time to witness this heinous crime.

Apparently, as we approached our house at breakneck speed with the 'helpers' shouting 'Dad, look what's happened', dad ignored the cries as he was busy taking off his wide leather belt and although Jack tried to justify what he'd done, pointing out my bloody leg and pleading his innocence, dad gave him a good hiding with the belt and a tongue lashing on the sanctity of the pitch, which Jack being the oldest son should have known better. I came second in importance, perhaps even less. Eventually our dad turned his attention to me and with a rag from his pocket he padded my gashed leg, it should have had stitches not a dirty rag and I was left there in the pram. Somehow Jack managed not to cry while others including me were bawling with pain or shock or fear of getting a dose of what Jack had been given. Meanwhile the 'helpers' had gone to tell our Mum as our dad went to inspect the damage done to his precious cricket table by the wheels of the rickety pram.

On reflection, I suspect that the 'scars' on dads' wicket (if they ever existed) would have disappeared within hours, whereas I still have the scar on my leg fifty years later. But the scar of that day goes a lot deeper and the lesson which I believe it to have been, was to be repeated again and again throughout my working life.

Strange as it may seem, my feelings for my father over what seemed a callous act, mellowed over the years, for the playing surface was also the groundsman's child, his offspring that he had created, nursed and become a major part of his life. It's not meant for bodies to meander aimlessly across, there are parks for that and even in a park you are often told to 'keep off the grass.' A sports field is meant for sport no more, no less and even then only by selected users, not some mob with a pram.

Donald with his father Patrick Gallacher, and brother Robert, on the field which Patrick transformed from a meadow into a sports ground behind White Hart Lane, Spurs ground, in Tottenham, London. c1923

1974

The year is marked by the Three-Day Week, two general elections, a state of emergency in Northern Ireland, extensive IRA bombing of the British mainland and Britain entered its first post-war recession (Wikipedia)

Meanwhile in sport:

April   Leeds United win their second Football League First Division title.

April   Manchester United are relegated from the Football League First Division.

May   Alf Ramsey, who guided the England national football team to victory in the 1966 FIFA World Cup, is dismissed by the Football Association.

May   Liverpool win the FA Cup for the second time, beating Newcastle United 3–0 in the Wembley final.

July   Don Revie, the manager of Football League champions Leeds United appointed as the new England manager

July   Bill Shankly, manager of FA Cup holders Liverpool, stuns the club by announcing his retirement after 15 years as manager.

By the way:

April   The 19th Eurovision Song Contest was held at the Dome in Brighton, Sweden wins with the song 'Waterloo', performed by ABBA.

Nov 74   McDonald's open their fst UK restaurant in Woolwich, Southeast London

May74   Don Gallacher applied for the job as Head Groundsman of the Empire Stadium Wembley

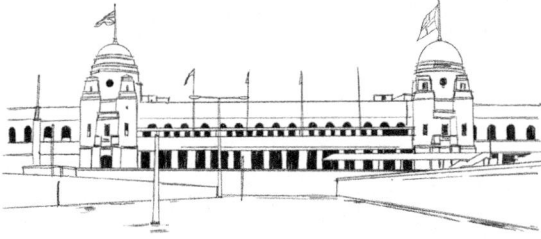

Chapter 1

The Road to Wembley May 1974

The long road approaching the Empire Stadium Wembley is called Olympic Way.

It's a long pedestrian roadway, which to my mind, captured the majesty of one of the most famous sporting arenas in the world and those that 'made it' to Wembley, even if only as a spectator. Might remember that as you approached the famous Twin Towers, the stadium appeared to grow wider and higher until you reached the steps and climbed humbly to its entrance. By which time you may have also appreciated the grandeur of this world-famous building and possibly the insignificance of yourself, as it had been in my case, on a number of occasions.

Then there was the emotion felt whilst climbing the broad steps, amongst a seething mass of people, passing through one of the turnstiles in its huge stone walls and crossing the cold concrete underground roadways know as 'The Level's, anxiously searching for a gate with a number to match a precious ticket clutched tightly in the hand. How precious was a 'Wembley Final' ticket? Through more gates, up or down even more steps until emerging from the shadows into a bright sky and a huge bowl of light, colour and noise, with at its centre, the greenest pitch many would have seen. Or so it will seem on that special day, for that was the Wembley Stadium effect, the ultimate sporting destination. You, the player, or the spectator would have 'arrived.'

The Empire Stadium Wembley, was a truly iconic place. Often representing the pinnacle of an individual's achievement in many sports, the goal of athletes at the top of their profession having beaten off tremendous opposition to get there. To the players, just striding across the pitch would be regarded as a milestone in any career, never to be forgotten. One legendary footballer when introduced to the pitch for the first time, is said to have thought someone was going tell them they couldn't play on it - the pitch was just too good – it was like a carpet, a bowling green.

Wembley Stadium was the venue most famous for staging cup finals in soccer, rugby and numerous international events, including the World Cup and the Olympic Games. I later learned that even mega-pop stars regarded Wembley as one of the few places in the UK where they could entertain more than 90,000 fans in one night and frequently did. It has been said that to perform in that stadium was the ultimate achievement for sports people, their clubs, their nations, their faithful supporters, and me.

Needless to say, it's only the winning teams, the most skilful players, the most famous performers, that will get to play at Wembley and presumably an objective very high on their list of must do. Likewise for their fans, and at a point, me.

Up until then I'd been lucky enough go to Wembley for a number of 'Cup Finals', and I'd made that walk alongside crowds of fans and shared the excitement, colour and noise created by 90,000 people, walking shoulder to shoulder, eager to see their team play in a cup-final, an international match or one of many other events.

But one afternoon in May 1974, I approached those Twin Towers along Olympic Way, all on my own, no big match to go to, no fans, no noise, and when I looked around, not even another pedestrian, just me.

I should add that the Olympic Way, only goes to Wembley Stadium, nowhere else. You have to have a reason and mine was, that I was applying for the number one job in my own career. You see, I was a groundsman at a college sports ground, right behind the Tottenham Hotspur Football stadium in North London, and I was going for the job as The Head Groundsman at Wembley Stadium, a quantum leap. Some said that I had ambitions way above my station, justifiably so considering my modest background. And no one knew that better than me, but I would soon learn whether or not I was kidding myself and I would happily take it on the chin when I got back home, but at least my name was in the hat.

On that memorable day in May, the Olympic Way was incredibly quiet and seemed to be a lot longer than I remembered and the stadium very much bigger by the time I reached the entrance, and this time without the need of a Cup Final ticket, just me looking for the general office.

I was only there because another groundsman had persuaded me to go after the Wembley job in the first place. My pal Henry Naylor had been Tottenham Hotspur's groundsman for many years and as well as being a good neighbour, what with the White Hart Lane stadium, being right next door to my somewhat less famous sports ground, he was a good friend and sometime mentor.

He'd seen the job advertised in 'The Groundsman' magazine

and made a point of calling me over to show me. I'd seen the advert too, but it hadn't occurred to me for a second to 'have a go', as Henry had put it, but he went on to convince me that I was as qualified as anyone, it was only one pitch after all, how difficult could it be?

He was of course stretching a point if not sending me up, but after a bit of thought, I decided I had nothing to lose by applying. So, I did and to my astonishment they wrote back inviting me for an interview and there I was, approaching Wembley Stadium, along Olympic Way, not believing for one minute that I might actually score.

From when I was about three years of age, helping my dad by raking grass, until I was in my fifties, I had been involved with the care of sports grounds. I had been many other things in between, turning my hand to whatever paid a wage, much as most people of my generation did. Some-time builder and decorator, mining coal or managing a sports goods warehouse. During the period in question, I had been employed by a large London Council, with responsibility for managing parks squares and everything horticultural in large chunks of its borough. Although born and bred in London, even I was surprised at just how many parks and squares there are, none of which looked after themselves. I make no bones about the fact that I was pleased to have the job and it was quite a challenge at first. I not only had the opportunity to organise manpower on a large scale, dealing with the planting and maintenance of thousands of trees. I also enjoyed being involved with shrubs, flowers and landscaping, no doubt passed down from my dad, just one of his many skills. Whilst there was a lot to make the role worthwhile, it wasn't keeping my interest, especially as local politics and bureaucracy became a constant feature of the job.

My real love was, and still is, all about sports grounds, always a challenge, sometimes a joy, often a curse.

My father, Patrick Gallacher, was born in Glasgow in 1881, and by 1902-03, was playing top class football for Duntocher Hibs. When offers from Sunderland, Hibernian and Tottenham Hotspur came in. He picked the latter but unable to maintain a first team spot with The Spurs so after one season, he moved to Luton Town. By which time he had met Alice Amelia Nicholson, who lived in her father's house at 7 Trulock Road, Tottenham, a stone's throw and in sight of the Tottenham Hotspur football ground. Which despite him playing for several other clubs across the British Isles during the following years, was to remain the family home for another 70 years.

When the First World War broke out, he was playing for Ton Pentre, a Welsh Club, but with the world in turmoil he joined the Footballers Battalion (17th Middlesex Regiment), where, in between the fighting across battlefields, he was also their player coach and responsible for procuring areas to use for the battalion to play matches against other regiments, in unimaginable conditions.

Back in North London, after the war, he was hired to create a sports field from a former nursery, a rough meadow, which filled the area between the family home at 7 Trulock Road and the Tottenham Hotspur football ground. The land had been purchased by St Ignatius, Jesuit college located a few miles away, chosen for students to play rugby or cricket. I can only imagine that after the battlefields of The Somme, turning a meadow into a sports ground would have been fairly straightforward. Myself and three more of my brothers were born in that house and as a consequence, we grew up with our very own 'park' on the Tottenham field. Being virtually weaned on grass, weather and seasons, and the importance that those elements meant in the world of groundmanship. Although I doubt we consciously thought about it. We certainly spent more time 'on the field' than we ever spent in the house, summer or winter. My father later went on to become an exceptional groundsman, at the original West Ham Stadium, London, and then a massive factory complex in Enfield, Middlesex. He knew his business, and we were his helpers, so we couldn't help but learn a lot.

I was one of six brothers who played most sports at a competitive level, although we mostly played for the sheer joy of it, especially cricket and football. Our Dad played for Partick Thistle, Tottenham Hotspur, Luton, Barrow & Workington amongst others. His sons played for Tottenham, West Ham, Leicester and Leyton Orient, through the post WW2 years and a host of good amateur clubs for long after.

We played sport in an era when it was perfectly natural for a player to replace a 'divot' in the ground, be it cricket, football or rugby. It was as natural as breathing in and out, for in those days, players - especially the youngsters - often had the job of helping the groundsman before and after a match or even training. Being the sons of a professional footballer and later a groundsman, our interest was invariably more second nature than most. My brother Bob and I took it seriously enough to take on the role full time later on, but all of the brothers had the knowledge through years of growing up and working on that field. So, a modest background, without a doubt, a wealth of experience? Well Henry thought I had and who was I to argue with the Head Groundsman of the Spurs ground?

Anyway, going by the job description, I was fairly confident that I could handle it. After all it was 'only one pitch' as I kept telling myself. But sitting at home analysing my chances was one thing, writing the application wasn't too much trouble either, but I do remember hesitating for a second, when it came to actually posting the letter in the box on the corner of our road, equal distance between my workplace and the Tottenham Hotspur ground.

However, by the time I entered the stadium for the actual interview, my confidence had lessened considerably, and the final few steps to the Wembley management offices were all the steeper for it. I could have, maybe should have, turned back at any time. Nothing lost, but then nothing would have been gained and I really did want to move on, so what the hell!

During my interview with the Assistant General Manager, I had to describe my background in great detail. Actually, listening to myself give a potted history in the life of a groundsman was rather interesting, well to me it was, I couldn't tell whether or not he did. I expect that I went on a bit, given any audience I usually do. The longer the conversation went on the more specific the questions became, the more I got into my stride and began to forget my nerves, including the fact that I was sitting in an office inside Wembley Stadium with the audacity to apply for the 'top job'.

To say the least, it was all a bit unreal. So when I was introduced to the General Manager and the Chief Engineer, my nerves had mostly disappeared and I felt as though I was just there for an interesting chat. This showed up particularly, when I was asked what I suspected at the time, was a 'trick' question, if not a a rather naive one.

"What type of fertiliser would you use on the Wembley pitch Mr. Gallacher?" – a long pause. "I couldn't tell you", I said. By this time, I was a bit full of myself. I had been talking my subject for a while, not theirs and whilst they doubtless knew a lot about Wembley Stadium, they clearly knew little or nothing about playing surfaces. "Or at least I won't name one" I said, "I wouldn't dream of prescribing a feed to go into any turf that I hadn't learned a lot about over a reasonable period of time – and that's more likely to be weeks than hours. In fact, I wouldn't expect to change much at all until I knew the ground like the back of my hand, and I most certainly wouldn't begin to tell you about your turf from a chair in this office and anyone who does is fooling himself."

I have never known when to shut up, as that remark seemed to go down like a lead balloon. In fact, the stony silence made me suspect that other candidates may well have offered the kind of answer that they expected, and I had gone too far as usual. I tried to recover what may have been a mistake and said something like "but I've really only been as close to the pitch as any other spectator and obviously haven't talked to anyone who actually knows the ground".

Another silence, then the boss said "Quite right. Well, let's straighten that out first". So shortly afterwards and somewhat relieved that *I'd got away with it,* I was shown the world famous, Wembley turf very close up indeed.

Just like most people, I had never been inside the stadium without thousands of other people to keep me company and whilst it was 'only one pitch' it looked pretty big in those first few moments walking out of the offices into the daylight to be introduced to some of the ground staff. On the famous turf I met Jack ('Jacky') Packham who had understudied (unofficially) the Head Groundsman Percy Young, for many years. Percy, who was retiring, was away that day and so it was left to Jacky to deputise, which he did very well. After a mini tour with plenty of questions and comments flying, mostly between myself and Jacky, who was very easy to get on with, we returned to the office of the General Manager. The various officials disappeared, leaving me with my thoughts until someone brought me a cup of tea. Very soon I was ushered into the outer office and quizzed on my current salary and the amount of notice required by my employers should the job be offered to me. Everything seemed as it should be and was winding down for me to go. Strange as it may seem, I had actually enjoyed myself, in fact, it had been a great day out. There would be lots to tell the family, blimey, I had walked out on the Wembley pitch for a start.

The office was a sizeable room and from where I was sitting, I couldn't really hear what was being said by the managers as they talked about something or other. In fact, I thought that something important, other than the subject of me had cropped up, until a kind of lull gradually came over their proceedings with what I thought to be a stand-off between them. So, looking for something to say if only so that I could get off home, I sort of coughed to get their attention and said, "Have you any idea when a decision might be made, you know, when I might hear from you?" "Hear from us? Oh, we want to give you the job Mr Gallacher, we intend to appoint you as groundsman, but we were just wondering if we could get your employer to waive the months' notice so you could start immediately. Would it be all right with you if we telephone them?"

Bang, right between the eyes, it wasn't the answer I'd expected. I hadn't really got used to the fact that I was actually sitting there in the first place. For one of the few occasions in my life I was lost for words. I suppose I'd expected to be sent a letter in the post like normal people do, perhaps get a phone call when they had considered all the candidates. What had never occurred to me was for anyone to say, "When can you start?" I just wasn't ready with an answer. It served me right for asking in the first place. But I must have mumbled some kind of reply, I don't really remember.

That was it then, Don Gallacher was the new Head Groundsman of Wembley Stadium and whether or not I previously had ideas above my station, it no longer mattered. I would now have to put my money where my mouth was and at the time, I seem to recall that it was hanging wide open with not a sound coming out.

What would my wife Betty ('Bet') say? What would the rest of the family think? Would Henry Naylor be surprised, or would he just say, 'I told you so'? Most likely the latter knowing Henry. A thousand things rushed through my head, none of which were particularly clear. Meanwhile the management who were oblivious to my state of mind still carried on talking between themselves, making phone calls and running a world-famous sports stadium I assumed. The little matter of appointing a new groundsman was completed.

Anyway, they couldn't reach my employer, but the job was mine, and after more handshaking and assurances of confirmation in the post, I eventually left the stadium offices and made my way down the steps, of which there seemed to be a lot more of them than when I had come in.

I suppose I was about halfway back along the Olympic Way (definitely a lot longer) toward the station. When I stopped, turnedand stared up at those famous Twin Towers trying to take it all in, I just stood there trying to take stock of what had just happened.

There I was at fifty-five, after a lifetime of grafting, the Head Groundsman of the premier sports ground in the country and among the most famous in the world. I had been a groundsman most of my working life, largely working on college playing fields, amateur sports clubs and one or two posh cricket grounds. The sort of places where the groundsman is typically regarded by many as the bloke in the rough clothes in the rough weather who keeps the grass down and the lines marked, with a wage packet just as short as the grass on a test wicket. Yet I'd gone and picked up the plum groundsman jobs - Wembley Stadium. You don't even have to say 'Stadium' when referring to it, the name Wembley doesn't usually conjure up the High Street or the railway station, lovely as I am sure they both are. It was a wee bit frightening. I had planned to go back to work after the interview, but it was getting late by then and it was the last place I wanted to go, I wasn't ready. On the journey home, the enormity of what had just occurred wouldn't sink in and I remember vividly wondering what the hell I'd let myself in for.

Well, it wasn't very long before I was to find out. In what became just one month's time I was to take over from a groundsman who was retiring after 40 years. In certain circles Percy Young had become something of a legend in his own right and his boots were going to take some filling. I didn't appreciate it then but there were to be plenty of times in the future when I was going to be, if not frightened, then certainly rattled and I am well known for being neither easily frightened nor easily rattled.

Wembley Stadium, along with Wimbledon, Lords and a few other grounds, rank amongst the most written about pieces ofgrass in the country. If you think about it, those particular playing surfaces have to be fantastic whenever they hold a special event, and that's the irony: every event is special. With most stadiums or sports grounds, the players or fans expect the ground to be wet after rain, dry during a drought and muddy patches appear after a long season. That wasn't acceptable at Wembley, Wimbledon or Lords, particularly when the media arrive, it's as though the event they cover on the day is the only one that's been held there that year. That part of the job was a hard one to get used to and was going to be in the background throughout my time in charge and I believe, continues today.

I also had a number of preconceived theories to explore regarding the Wembley pitch which was going to make life interesting for me too. Having played a bit of football on many a dodgy ground and managed a good amateur football team on even worse, I had often thought that the 'sacred turf' of Wembley might be made a better playing surface, whatever the sport. It was well known that at its best it was a joy to behold and must have been fantastic for the ball players especially. At its worst, it had sometimes been little more than a quagmire when lesser grounds on the same day were playable. Not so simple to implement though, I was to discover that it wasn't my job to get creative and certainly wasn't the role of any ordinary groundsman. After all, Wembley wasn't a sports ground, this was a Sports Arena with all those things and more.

I'll say there were more: greyhound racing twice a week; world speedway championships; rugby; football; hockey; hurling; Gaelic football; musical cavalcades; pop concerts; Live Aid, and even the likes of the stunt man Evel Knievel with ramps right across the pitch from corner to corner leaping over thirteen buses.

For much of my adult life I had prepared most types of sporting surfaces. From athletics to soccer, cricket, rugby and the like and to make them as perfect as conditions and my skills could possibly make them. I had done this for top class cricketers or for a bunch of toffee-nosed schoolboys. (Often, it was for top class schoolboys or a bunch of toffee-nosed cricketers, but that's by the way.) This was very different. I was to learn that every event was to be a 'Final' with thousands of eyes towards the field of play, and with television of course, that became millions.

The supporters or reporters will always remember that last time they were at Wembley the grass was 'much shorter' or 'longer' or 'greener' or whatever met their ideal. Before a match, when the commentators or pundits on the day ran out of script, the conversation would sometimes be directed at the pitch. Typically, 'Well Brian, I've been on the pitch today and in my opinion it's alright', or 'all wrong' often depending on what he thinks is expected of him as much as his professional opinion. The public won't be aware (and why should they be anyway), that the previous week the pitch was marked out for rugby or hockey, not soccer, and maybe the following day hundreds of guardsmen with dirty great big boots would cover the pitch marching over the lush turf; brass instruments, mascot and all and still it had to look perfect for the next event which again may only be a matter of days later.

During the next few years, I was to learn that being an expert in my field (pardon the pun) was not enough. I was to be a diplomat to one and all, sometime politician; negotiator; interviewee for the media and target for every self-appointed expert who had a wealth of experience with nothing more than a lawn mower but significant access to a soap box.

By any standards The Empire Stadium Wembley, for whatever the occasion is impressive. I'd obviously enjoyed the times I had been a spectator. Then and now I'd shared in the emotion of the supporters who, as they settle themselves in a seat, turns to his or her neighbour, often with a strong dialect and say something like 'We're here then, we made it to Wembley'. 'We', being the achievement by the supporters as much as the team. It's often as though the occasion makes the game of secondary importance to actually 'getting there' and unfortunately that's what some of them become - the games didn't always live up to expectations. Perhaps it's Wembley that does it, puts them off I mean. I'm told that even experienced international players go a bit lightheaded as they run out of the players' tunnel. That to most sports men or women, the day of the match, is naturally a day of tension and butterflies, but when the acoustics of the stadium echo to more than 80,000 voices it sounds like hell let loose, seemingly directed at each individual player. Probably less so for the experienced, but what chance a young lad, who last week when taking a throw-in, was so close to the crowd he could feel the spectator's breath on his backside and hear every remark made. Good, bad and really bad. On the touchline at Wembley, I am told you can hear them all right, but you can't see them, not individuals, just one enormous presence, one gigantic roar, the 'Wembley Roar' of fans cheering their team predominantly from one end or the other as though of one voice. It must be unnerving, especially for the less experienced - at least at first - and believe me, when the stadium is empty, the silence is just as loud and has a similar effect on the uninitiated.

I can still remember how this 'young lad' felt, looking up at the world-famous Twin Towers as I left the stadium on the day of my interview - not unlike any young superstar I would imagine. But just like them I wouldn't have admitted that it was a touch of nerves or apprehension that made my heart flutter on the day, I was just a bit breathless that's all. I reckon it must have been the long uphill struggle that enables anyone to get to Wembley that does it, what do you think?

**Olympic Way, Wembley Stadium,
London c1960**

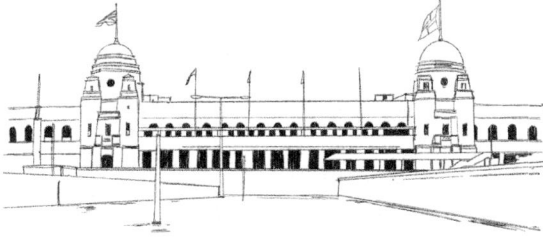

Chapter 2

Eyes Open & Mouth Shut

In fact, it took a lot longer to begin work there than anyone had hoped, reporting for work in October 1974, just before a big international football match: England against Czechoslovakia. Percy Young, the retiring groundsman had kept me close to him so as to explain the many things that made up a typical day's work, as though anything at Wembley Stadium could be typical or normal. This involved a fair bit of 'hanging about' and I must confess to being a bit impatient at the time.

I would have preferred to have worked alongside the ground staff a lot more and just quiz Percy during breaks and suggested so, especially with what he had on his plate.

I felt that he didn't need me shadowing him all over the place, but that's how it's done for most jobs, just standard practice. I probably thought that I didn't need too much practice, just dive in, which would be a typical Don Gallacher attitude.

From what I could see, Percy had plenty of other things to worry about. With time running out, he had the big international match coming up with a very wet pitch and no sign of the rain abating.

17

This was October 1974, and we were in for one of the wettest winters in recorded history. Upwards of thirty labourers were on the pitch, forking the ground out to about 20 feet from the edge of the turf. The whole of the area on both sides of the pitch was a real quagmire. The ground staff used every trick available to them, even resorting to squeegees (sponges), but with little obvious effect. The main body of the pitch was wet, but in places, the sides were actually under water.

It didn't stop Jacky Packham from cutting the grass though, just as he always did about that time before a match. He had a system, and he was sticking to it, even though when he reached the sides the mower took on the appearance of a boat ploughing through a lake producing a bow wave. Absolutely ridiculous, but he kept going regardless - and still the rain came down. In fact, the rain was relentless throughout the build-up and when match day dawned it was still coming down.

At a point and in an effort to give protection, Percy had the sides of the pitch covered in polythene sheeting, but with little benefit to show for the enormous effort. Whilst such tactics obviously protect it from the rain it wouldn't allow the playing surface to dry out naturally and anyway, the damage was already done by that time.

Undeterred, by mid-afternoon the sheets were removed, and Percy marked the pitch. In some places the marking machine was struggling so badly it couldn't create a white line, it was simply skidding in the mud making a dirty white smear. The solution was to get stadium staff painters to finish the lines with 2' paint brushes albeit using the same whiting compound obviously - and still it rained.

Meanwhile for much of the time I observed, I was still 'the new boy', and remembered some good advice from my old man who had told me, that there are times when its best to keep my eyes open and my mouth shut, at least for the time being. So be it.

At the top of the players' tunnel at 8am that morning Percy had met the ground staff and said, 'Right lads' and as far as I could tell, that's the only instruction he gave all day and yet they all went about their respective jobs, not all of which were to do with the pitch. It seemed that they all knew their roles and routine backwards. I was full of admiration throughout the day: watching the procedure that seemingly happened at every big event at Wembley. It was all so 'matter of fact'.

I have been in the crowd plenty of times, mostly football matches, but even I hadn't noticed the changes made for an event, most of which was the transition from the evening dog racing which I wouldn't have been aware of anyway. For example, all the floodlight lamp posts around the dog track were removed and hundreds of seats put back in the area on the North Side (Royal Box) where the bookmakers and punters would usually stand on dog nights.

A huge ramp was placed across the dog track like a bridge, so as not to damage the turf (dog track). The weight of the ramps was also ridiculous, it took four strong men to lift them, and some were hurt doing it. Nonetheless, it seemed to go like clockwork. All this impressed me no end and made me feel a little better when anticipating the time when it would be my responsibility, not just an observer. It looked as though I would have an established team to back me up and I would merely have to say, 'right lads' and it would all fall into place - nothing to it!

Unfortunately, the theory broke down in a big way before it was put into practice. A key member of the team, Jacky Packham, who had been there for thirty years and deputised for Percy during holidays and sickness. He was the bloke with the mower-cum-motorboat, and cutting the pitch both ways involved walking that machine for several miles for each event. Well, with the combination of rain; that horrible cold concrete stadium and quite possibly his roll-up fags, it became obvious he could hardly breathe. Typical of the dedicated groundsman, this hard-headed man desperately tried to carry on. Percy and I were very concerned about him, but Percy said that Jacky was the most obstinate of men (not his actual words) something I would have to understand when I wanted to get his co-operation in the future. It was very good advice, but that time Jacky lost the fight and ended up in hospital with double pneumonia and in a very bad way.

The evening of the international match went off without a hitch and my apprehension about the state of the pitch was unnecessary, in fact the conditions were hardly mentioned. Of course not, in all the activity I'd completely missed the point. The ninety minutes of football was what it was all about, not the weeks of preparation, not the skill, sweat and worry, not even the dedication that puts a man in hospital. What had been important to everyone involved was to create the best setting possible, but spectators didn't come to look at the stage, the spectators went to see the performers on it. The fact that England beat the Czechs three - nil may have helped I suppose, but that's by the way. None the less, I was surprised that the condition of the pitch, the world famous, sacred turf, just didn't live up to its image and wondered what I had inherited.

One of the questions I am often asked is whether or not I enjoy the matches and up to that first big match, I would have replied very positively. But I soon learned that for most of the officials and staff on duty, although we watch the games in a piecemeal sort of way and enjoy the atmosphere, the games are just a small part, almost an anti-climax compared to what goes on before, during and afterwards. Particularly that night, I think I was watching almost everything but the game, someone else told me the score and I didn't even get a programme to take home, much to my kid's annoyance.

Another learning curve and a responsibility that was a bit strange to me was greyhound racing, which as I have mentioned, was held twice and sometimes three times a week. It also meant the dog owners holding trials midweek during the day. Now that had its moments. You should see the way the owners guard their dogs from prying eyes and presumably from being 'nobbled'. Blimey, James Bond doesn't come near it. I suppose, as gambling and big money is involved, secrecy is vital.

When I first went to Wembley, the dog track was grass, which cut up very badly on the bends as you might imagine with half a dozen dogs racing for position. You must have seen the posters that portray the dogs charging straight at you, leaning into the bends at a 45-degree angle. So, replacing the torn turf after every meeting was an important job because greyhound racing was important to the stadium as well as the paying public. Dog owners and punters could be as critical about their 'playing surface' as any player on the pitch. So, we had our own nursery in the stadium complex, cultivating the turf for just this purpose. But sometimes we couldn't cope and resorted to buying turf in from outside growers.

After a few years, I stopped getting annoyed but at first I did find it a bit rich when told that some turf supply companies, albeit quite correctly, were claiming to be 'Suppliers of turf to Wembley

21

Stadium' when actually it was only being used for the dog track to last for about a fortnight by which time the turf had been torn to shreds again. I did sometimes wonder how many proud gardeners across the UK managed to get a lawn looking as good as a dog track, which they thought was supposed to look like the sacred turf of Wembley. Quite a few I would imagine, but they probably believed that it was them that had somehow laid it wrong and not the supplier stretching the truth a little to boost their own image.

Many years ago, my father – who had taught me so much of my craft – had for a time been the groundsman at the original West Ham Stadium where they held greyhound racing. In fact, I understand that the stadium was built for greyhound racing not just football. And although I really hadn't been old enough or interested enough to have taken much in, I do remember him telling us tales of the racing fraternity. Dog racing in those days was a very big business, and the way he told it, had 'Chicago' style villains to exploit it, especially in the bigger cities. He would tell us stories about the East End racing gangs that made Al Capone sound like Snow White and her little friends, perhaps a bit exaggerated, but he made it sound very real. With that in mind, I tended to keep the latter day 'villains' at arm's length and spent my first greyhound meeting just standing in the crowd watching from the terraces to see what the staff did.

The routine seemed straightforward enough, in fact it puzzled me why the head groundsman had to be in attendance at all, but that was another tradition established for a long time. There were plenty of such oddities, not so unusual in a traditional organisation, but as things appeared to be running smoothly I wasn't going to interfere so early in the game. I was still 'the new boy' and tried to keep my eyes open and my mouth shut, at least for the time being.

At that time of the year, it was heavy with events at Wembley and another European Championship football match was imminent, England-v-Portugal and needless to say, it was still raining. The wings of the pitch by this time looked like Southend-on-Sea after the tide had gone out. Once more the fork and 'wellie' brigade were out and all the paraphernalia that it takes to combat the wet menace - and although it looked no worse than any other ground in the country, it wasn't looking a bit like the glossy pictures of Wembley.

In fact, my looking at the condition of club grounds on television gave me a whole new reason for watching 'Match of the Day'. Most grounds looked like ploughed sandy fields and I felt sorry for the poor devils that were fighting to maintain them. But not as sorry as I was at the pitiful mess I supervised during the repairing of Wembley the morning after the England-v-Portugal match: watching the ground staff replacing divots and filling holes was little better than kids playing mud pies. It was a terrible mess, and with yet another game just around the corner the rain came down unmercifully.

The conditions were grim, making every task more difficult. The time had come for a good talk with the ground staff to see how to get the best out of a poor lot. I was lucky to have good people on the ground in George McElroy and Reg Barwick, both twenty-year men, and Pat Sweeney, a wonderful bloke, ex-Irish Guards but very reliable despite that (just kidding, I am an Old Coldstream Guardsman), plus a couple of the lads, a formidable team to tackle this job.

We had a good talk, I laid out my plans, everyone said they understood and all we had to do then was to get on with it, because the next game was in fact very different: Percy had gone off to his

23

retirement and Jacky was still in the hospital, so this one was down to me. I hoped Father (God rest him) was paying attention, his boy may need some divine intervention.

© Thomas FEIGE | Dreamstime.com   © Alamy Stock Photos

The winter of 1974, a very wet period for all sports grounds across the country

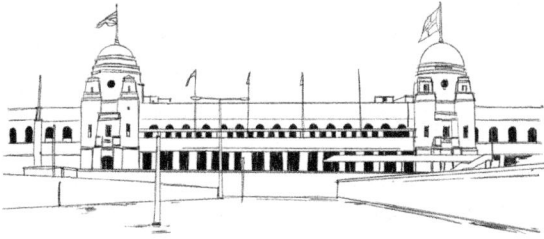

Chapter 3

Rain, Rain, Go Away

As previously mentioned, the winter of '74 had been the wettest on record up to that time, and all over the country, League club groundsmen were phoning around on a rumour that someone or other had found turf somewhere that didn't resemble a suet pudding, that's how scarce it was. But it had to be found and like them I too telephoned contacts and old pals and looked at any turf that was physically available, even though most places supplying turf were under water themselves, but almost anything was better than the slush that I had to work with.

It seemed a hopeless task, made more difficult by the standards that I obviously had to maintain. If I was to find 'sacred turf' in these conditions it looked like I was going to have to bless it myself and despite rumours to the contrary I hadn't yet been ordained.

Eventually in a little place in Buckingham I found just enough grass to work on. Roughly 4,000 pieces of what had once been the outfield of a village cricket ground, was with a little magic, going to become part of one of the most famous pitches in the world, a bit ironic. The turf was far from ideal, but as a substitute for mud and slurry they looked smashing to me.

So, I prepared the pitch for Oxford-v-Cambridge, that's the Varsity match, not the boat race. I know I keep on about it but they couldn't really have rowed along the sides of the pitch. The Varsity Match is an annual fixture played between the universities and by tradition, the match is held on the second Tuesday of December. Measured, marked and with just the goal posts to go up the officials declared that the playing surface was up to standard, and the game could go on.

But it had been touch-and-go, and I was even more determined to do something about the supposedly sacred turf after the game. With a couple of events under my belt I felt more able to demand answers of the establishment, I listened while I was told once again that a drainage system couldn't be laid under the sides because of the speedway track. Why the hell not? said I, it couldn't be that difficult and I'll tell you what I was told later on.

Meanwhile the events would go on, so temporary repairs were thrashed out with the contractors that did the heavy jobs at Wembley and work started in the first week of January 1975. What a mess though, despite using a bulldozer to lift the six inches of soil, we never seemed to progress more than about eighteen feet at a time because the rain hardly stopped, and the area being worked on was constantly being turned into a heap of sludge. It was bulldozed, pegged out, soil tipped and graded, trodden and turfed at breakneck speed hoping to beat the next downpour and usually failing.

I was once again counting the days off to the next big match and so were the blokes taking book on the big man with the big mouth not making it. But as usual this just made me even more determined to complete it in time and sure enough by the middle of February the pitch was in my opinion, ready to be played on.

Therefore giving it plenty of time to bed in and hopefully stay dry for the showpiece match on the 1st of March.

The League Cup Final that year was between Aston Villa and Norwich City, two gutsy teams that played determined football and compared to what they'd been playing on up and down the country I suspect that Wembley was wonderful. But compared to Wembley, Wembley was a bit average; at least to me it was. So, I closed my eyes a bit when sliding tackles tore yard long divots out of the surface and opened them to applaud the players putting them back before getting on with their match. It was a good game, and the losers didn't lose through my wet pitch and that was a relief.

This time we had managed to get the pitch as near to perfection as the conditions allowed but it had been uphill all the way. It had only been a stopgap as far as I was concerned though as near to perfection as I wanted, it would never happen until the whole playing area was well drained. Fortunately, even the management were convinced that a proper job was urgent and needed to move off of the drawing board. If the rain continued into the busy period we would have been in big trouble and even in those days there were calls for building a national stadium elsewhere. Such proposals were more often related to criticism of the building itself, outdated facilities, poor seating and dressing rooms and there was little mention of my pitch, but it wasn't worth feeding the critics with more ammunition than necessary.

On reflection I believe that the early period of pressure helped me to get to know the people I was to work with more quickly than would have happened otherwise and a mutual respect developed, a major factor in my success or failure later on. The General Foreman at the time was Peter Seddon and the Stadium Foreman Arthur Rose, both gave me a lot of support helping to fill the gaps that confronted me. My technical knowledge of the ground and all that grows in the Wembley complex was no problem. I'd been well trained for that but preparing for events was still a bit of a mystery and I found the help from all the foremen invaluable. Peter Seddon and I worked well together and had regular meetings to discuss the day-to-day workings, particularly my areas of responsibility.

One of the big differences to anything I had previously experienced was the rapid change of pitch layouts over a short period of time. Unless you are a follower of every conceivable sport, the events held at Wembley are whatever you read in the news or follow on the television, which of course included me before I took on the job.

Gaelic games, International Hockey, Rugby League and Soccer - I'd never had to change pitches so quickly in my life. My previous experience involved gradual, dare I say 'seasonal' changes from rugby or soccer to cricket and athletics, but I'd always had a couple of weeks in which to do it. At Wembley we might hold three different sporting events in as many weeks.

One of the things that we did when this happened was to set out high pressure hoses to wash out the unwanted lines. Very occasionally, if it was really bad we resorted to using green vegetable dye, but as little as possible and only on the lines that might cause confusion during a game. I've been accused of using dye, green sand and even green sawdust to cover up muddy patches, holes and weeds but that lush green turf of mine isn't fake and it looks the way it does as a result of damned hard work. But the trouble is that big brother, the TV cameras high in the roof, can see the unwanted lines. From up there, where no mortal should get to, the camera can see every shade of green, tiny daisies, weeds, any blemish or line that couldn't possibly confuse players on the ground, or the referee which is what our job is about. In fact, there were times when I would like to have had access to such microscopic scrutiny, it would have been very useful. But that all-seeing eye has a voice which it used to great effect, and when it talks, the world and my boss listened, so it's better that the lines are blotted out, high pressure hoses or green dye.

As I became more familiar with the role of Head groundsman, I began to make one or two breaks with tradition. Like many institutions some methods of working happened simply because 'it had always been done that way'. I am a great believer in tradition but just because it 'has always been done that way', doesn't necessarily make it right or even appropriate. Some traditional methods of working were less obvious than others, but one that irritated me was that of uniform. Since when should anyone wear a uniform in my line of work? Well on greyhound racing nights the Head Groundsman had to change into a smart uniform with a peaked cap and all the ground staff wore a uniform too. I didn't like the idea of looking like a commissionaire much, it wasn't me, anyway I doubt if they would have had my hat size. No one could tell me why I had to be there at all, let alone wear a uniform for a dog race when it was perfectly acceptable to wear an anorak in front of the Royal Box at a cup final. This was some kind of throwback to a time long past, so I rebelled and finally agreed to wear a white coat during races and continued to wear everyday clothes for big matches (I didn't really own an anorak).

Another break from tradition which didn't please everyone was that I chose to go into the men's mess at breaks and have a cup of tea and a joke or a moan. This will doubtless seem trivial but it's something I have always done believing it showed me to be the same as anyone else, human (which I nearly am). You learn more about a man in that environment than you do elsewhere, because for a while you are one of them and the truth and their opinions good or bad will out over a cup of tea and a break. I saw little point in being aloof from the men that you work with although some people do, including my predecessor. I chose not to conform and believe that it contributed to the kind of co-operation I got from the blokes later on, especially when the chips were down. But in some quarters it was frowned upon, 'good heavens taking tea with men, whatever next?' Hard luck, this is me and this is who was hired to get the job done.

So far so good. Although I was pleased with what had been achieved. I would have liked more changes from the outset, but it would take time to hack away at the solid establishment. In any large organisation there are people inwardly screaming to make changes to improve things, but there are always an equal number avoiding change, perhaps for a quiet life, to some it's an affront to their position. It's nothing new, it seems to me that in all walks of life individuals shut themselves away from knowledge or common sense and so as not to show their ignorance they sometimes stifle progress when they could gain so much more by harnessing the talent around them. I guess I was lucky, my parents taught their sons to admit their ignorance on a subject to those who know better, that way we learn from them. If we bluffed it, our ignorance would be rumbled soon enough, and they may not let on that they know what you don't.

With this in mind I adopted the routine of talking through each job that I gave to the ground staff. I didn't want them doing tasks 'parrot fashion' and equally they often pointed out flaws or better ways of doing things. We usually ended up doing it my way, but that's the governor's prerogative, at least they knew why and we all gained knowledge each time. In this way one or two good men who may have held back went from Wembley to top clubs where they had an opportunity to blossom. I hoped that I helped to get them there in the same way that many people have helped me along the way too.

Get off your hobby horse Gallacher, you can't beat them, you don't want to join them, so like everyone else, you just have to grin and bear it.

Three Wise Men (of turf) trying to find any grass worth using on their own saturated grounds.

Don Gallacher,
Head Groundsman
Wembley Stadium

Frank Brittan,
Turf Consultant,
T. Parker & Sons

Jim Thorne,
Head Groundsman,
Wimbledon All England & Lawn Tennis Club

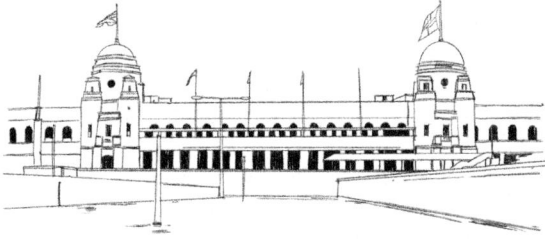

Chapter 4

Hallowed Turf?

I began this memoir by relating the story of when I was a toddler, playing with my brothers on the edge of our dads sports field, I tripped and fell on a scythe, slicing my shin almost to the bone, and my brother Jack used a rickety pushchair to take me home to get me urgent help. So urgent it took him and the pram with me bleeding profusely in it, right across dad's precious cricket table. Unfortunately, our dad, the groundsman, had seen this heinous crime and gave his eldest son a harsh lesson with his belt.

I have also expressed how my feelings for my father may have mellowed over the years, as I came to appreciate that the playing surface was also the groundsman's creation and a major part of his life, it's not meant for bodies to meander aimlessly across. It's a problem that all groundsmen have because the preparation care and attention are not usually appreciated by mere mortals any more than potential damage to a playing area.

This problem gained momentous proportions at Wembley, particularly with visiting International teams, requiring 'practice' the evening before a match. But they weren't on their own. TV crews and film makers always seem to have a lot of 'helpers', who apparently are there for the day out as they don't always appear to serve any particular purpose.

There have been photographers and even security men kicking a ball about before the game, presumably to go home and crack a joke about playing at Wembley, but it was no joke to me. I honestly never worry if it's 22 players or 1,000 bandsmen and women, whereas just one clown, is one pair of boots too many. Some of the time, in fact most of the time, it wouldn't matter a jot, but it does depend on what we have done to the surface in the way of preparation or maintenance at that time.

An example of this happened when Jacky and I were returning from lunch one day and we saw quite a lot of people wandering about an area of the pitch, clearly no one that we knew. 'What the bloody hell's this'? I thought, and being the quiet mannered sort of chap that I am, I grudgingly suppressed my anger, (after all they're innocent until proven guilty, aren't they?). Then, by the time that we reached the edge of the pitch I'd decided not to murder more than about half of them. But as Jacky and I approached, one character in the group started waving frantically in our direction shouting; "Oi you, move out of the bloody way ". and just like a scene from a 'Carry On' film, Jacky and I both looked behind us believing someone else was following, before realising that he was shouting at us.

And I so liked the "Oi", we were obviously up against an intellectual here. A few more yards and we got a repeat performance, waving even more frantically and shouting, "Oi, are you bloody deaf or something? You're in the way." By this time, we'd realised that they were filming something or other and somehow we were in the shot. Also, by then I had recognised a number of minor television personalities among the film crew who had stopped whilst the new interruption took its course. The merchant shouting 'Oi' was obviously not used to interruption especially from the likes of us and when we reached the group I addressed him quietly, which wasn't at all what I felt like, I was boiling inside. I said, "and who gave you permission to do whatever it is you're doing?"

The 'mouthy' one, obviously put out, replied slowly and patronisingly 'we have the permission of the General Manager, who said we could film on the pitch once we get the O.K. from the groundsman, a Mr. Gallacher, now will you please move over to the side'.

"Really" said I, "But you're already on the pitch, by the bloody dozen and I know for a fact that you haven't spoken to Mr. Gallacher yet". "No, well, we thought we'd get set up and save time while we wait for him". Couldn't make this up could you?

"Setting up for what, War & Peace part two? Well, my talkative friend, it's not your bloody day, the Mr Gallacher you want is me. It's obviously nothing more than a twenty quid documentary that wasn't even scheduled with us. So now you can try and convince me who needs to be involved and if your powers of persuasion are better than your manners, they might get to stay. The rest can get off my pitch, starting now" (getting loud). He didn't like it much, well he wouldn't, would he? Despite his protestations especially when Jacky waded into them somewhat menacingly, the bodies and hangers on were thinned out quite rapidly.

We obviously had plenty of television film crews working on the ground, especially on match days and I got along with most of them. As a rule, they were professional tight knit teams with a job to do and I've seen what they need in way of numbers. This was just one obnoxious character, possibly making a name for himself and an enormous entourage wandering about all over the place. Anyway, he ended up with the principal people, cameraman, sound man, director and so on and of course the principal presenters concerned. The others got my version of 'Oi you' and despatched to the stands a bit quick.

There were many incidents like that, some I have mentioned later in the book, some are significant most are not, but however important or otherwise these incidents are to me, they are not in the least bit important to the perpetrators.

There are dozens of reasons why a groundsman cannot bear to see odd bods out for a stroll on his turf, and his concern will never be understood really because in the main the belief is that grass is grass is grass, well it isn't. Believe it or not, the cultivation of turf has become an exact science, especially in recent years with places like Wembley Stadium requiring specific varieties of grasses fed with specific minerals and fertilisers to cope with specific conditions and tasks. The average person sees the sacred turf of Wembley as a rather 'super' version of their own lawn, a sort of nice green colour with stripes in it. Unfortunately, the average person doesn't know much about their own lawn either, but that's by the way.

I'll give you a couple of examples. One weekday, a visitor came to see me and found his way in by walking up the player's tunnel, the outer gates being open for deliveries and such. He had his dog on a lead by his side, obviously very well behaved, but a dog. The visitor spotted me at the opposite end of the pitch, so he whistled and shouted out to attract my attention and just as I did look up, the dog crouched down in the distant penalty area and peed on the grass, not exactly on the penalty spot but near enough.

Unfortunately, at that distance my shouts and frantic waving didn't get the offending creature (or his dog) off of the pitch and all I managed to do was confuse the visitor who, having patiently waited for his dog to finish, was continuing his walk towards me, straight down the middle, penalty area, through centre spot, to penalty area. Now this chap is a very sensible down to earth character with a lot of common sense and a great respect for the place he was in. I would go so far as to say he was at the time in awe of the place. Yet it still hadn't occurred to him the extent of damage that he had allowed his beloved dog to do. That simple, seemingly most natural function was allowed to occur by the unthinking visitor, because to him and presumably his dog, grass is grass is grass. Even if it's 'posh' grass with nice stripes and despite my urgent attention to repairing the then scorched turf, my groundsman's eye could see the spot where the poor dog crouched for many weeks later. My only consolation was that for months later I reminded him of his dreadful crime every time I saw him. He didn't bring his beloved dog back for a re-run.

Another incident that comes to mind concerned a couple of people on the stadium staff who should have known a lot better and in fairness did from time to time show their awareness of the need to keep off the pitch, to the extent that they often had conversations with me by shouting from the side lines rather than just walking out to wherever I was standing. These were some of the chaps who had heard me explain to the uninitiated, the problems of spreading fungus and disease about the turf by the simple act of walking on it at the wrong time and very few people could possibly know when that might be.

None-the-less these same two didn't appreciate why I bawled them out when I saw them take a short cut across the pitch one winter when it had several inches of snow on it. They believed, like many others, that it couldn't possibly do any harm, how could it? Well, it was sometime after the snow had gone that I was able to show them and a few others, the footprints on the turf where their size 10's had compressed and melted the snow, forming into ice, freezing and killing the grass below.

A simple, natural, unthinking act, made by people supposedly in the know, gave me spots before the eyes and them a metaphorical kick up the rear, but they still thought it was a bit over the top. Like I said, 1,000 marching bandsmen in army boots and a goat as a mascot is perfectly alright by me. But 1,000 bandsmen, in the Military Pageant, a goat (mascot) and one clown, is one clown too many.

In this book I don't intend to get technical on the methods of keeping the Wembley turf sacred because it would become even more boring than necessary. Suffice to say that the days of the groundsman in a cloth cap and straw sticking out of his ear are long past, if they ever existed at all. Today whether he's looking after the most famous ground in the land or a school playing field, the skills and the knowledge expected of the groundsman is far greater than he is generally given credit for by anyone other than his peers. More importantly the demands made on a pitch today are far greater than ever before and it's true that grass left to its own devices will grow and recover quite well, but only if you don't have 22 players, cricketers, tennis stars or a few hundred schoolboys playing on it over prolonged periods. Then it needs help, ideally by people that know what they're doing.

The term 'hallowed turf' generally refers to the Wembley Stadium pitch and its association with the final of the FA Cup played there. Hallowed means holy and turf is a reference to the grass or pitch so fans see Wembley as holy ground, or so I'm told.

But even 'holy' grass that's allowed to grow on its own, is usually called a field, you often see animals grazing on it. The turf that I am concerned with doesn't need any more hindrance than necessary, so unless you've earned the right to be on the Wembley pitch, or you've been invited, the message is simple: Keep off!

Don Being interviewed for TV prior to a big match

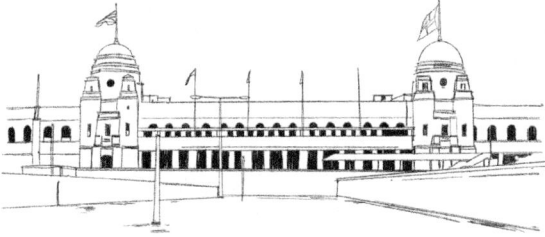

Chapter 5

Going to the Dogs

Wembley Stadium had been a regular venue for greyhound racing since the first race held there back in 1927 and although the number of spectators became a shadow of what it was in its heyday, it was still very popular with the punters and an important source of income for the stadium. Not as popular with me when I first started as I had to be in attendance during the two evenings each week that the meetings took place. But that was just inconvenience and nothing compared to the effort needed for the maintenance of the greyhound track.

One early Saturday morning, in bitter cold miserable weather, the rain belting down and Wembley was about as appealing as a pair of wet socks, which we soon had. I arrived as usual at about 7.30 a.m. and had a slow walk around to the mess room to find George McElroy already there and brewing up, he must get there about 6 a.m. He forced a cup of tea into my hand which was just the ticket and one by one the seven other lads rolled in. You could tell by their faces that they were already eager to get stuck into a day on the dog track, a miserable task at the best of times, this wasn't one of those, this was the winter of 1974-75, known in our circles as 'the wet one'.

I've made a lot of how the pitch was nearly ruined that winter, well the greyhound track suffered the same conditions and the dog racing held twice a week was a darned sight more damaging than some of the twinkle toed footballers could ever cause. The claws of the dogs tear up the turf really badly especially on the bends where they dig in to gain advantage on each other. I keep hearing of some dogs being 'wide runners' but you wouldn't think so to look at the track after the event because it's usually only about four feet from the fence at each bend that suffers the most damage. Just there you'd believe a ruddy great cultivator had been preparing the ground for vegetables. Anyway, whatever else was happening, it meant that almost every weekend was devoted to making good the damage by repairing and re-turfing using turves taken from the stadium nursery.

By the eight o'clock start everyone was ready at the players tunnels where the tools were kept, but me, being me said, "hold on let's have a look at the methods we're using to do this job". I got the usual moans and groans that I'd come to expect. No great surprise as the job had been done this way for donkey's years and every time Don said, 'hold on let's have a look,' it meant change and nobody likes to change. George was downright rude, but then he thought everyone was an idiot at the time, and anyone who'd been there less than thirty years was a novice. That sort of thing never bothered me one bit. It had to be expected in the early days in charge, at least until the few changes I'd made had proven their worth, and well, this nonsense with the dog track was an obvious candidate for change.

The method they had used up to that time started on a Saturday morning with the ground staff cutting out the damaged turves and lifting them onto a lorry. Disposing of it outside and whilst the new turf was being loaded, two men would clean up and grade the area ready for when the others came back. This was repeated on the Sunday when the casuals came in and to all intents and purposes, it seemed to work fine. A gang managed to lay about 250 turves each weekend which wasn't bad considering the turf has to go down accurately and be fit for use in a few days. It may be just a dog track but it was Wembley's dog track. Every turf had to be cut precisely, laid and kicked in so it was just a question of getting on with it until the job was done. What method there might have been had mostly come from habit, not a lot of planning or design.

I'd watched this for a few weekends and came up with my own version, if I was wrong all that would be lost would be a bit of face, mine. So, on that occasion we'd do it my way. We started on the fourth bend, a real mess it was that day. With heavy board and an edging iron, George cut the outside edge of the section I'd chosen to repair; turves were cut into 12' squares and lifted on to a lorry which took what was by then muddy green rubbish to be dumped. One of the most difficult parts of the job at this point is when you try to hold the turfing iron, fork or shovel in one hand and hold your nose with the other. I couldn't begin to describe the dreadful smell that hit you as the wretched clods of grass were disturbed. This was a dog track, and the greyhounds may be house trained but they're not fussy about using our grass track as an enormous toilet although how it can occur at over 30 mph is still a mystery to me.

Leaving two of the lads to continue with the grading we walked outside through the player's tunnel and passed the kennels. The general area there was in a terrible state, there were no concrete car parks at that time and just an old hardcore roadway running

43

down to the old turf nursery where good old Paddy was waiting with an equally old Bedford truck. We loaded it with about 300 turves, these were tough 'sods', good fibre, absolutely useless near the pitch or a nice lawn but just right for the greyhound track and you don't have to be gentle with them either, which was just as well as we weren't.

Paddy turned the lorry around and I told them to throw about a cubic yard of sand on board which was new to them, then he drove back to the stadium up through the player's tunnel and over the ramps. We unloaded the turf, and the lads began to spread the sand over the prepared surface. The sand was to serve two purposes, one it would give a better draining effect, secondly when it came to lifting the turves again as we surely would, the job would be a damned sight easier. By the end of the day I was getting quite happy with what had been achieved: the track was ready to be turfed and 330 turves were stacked alongside the track ready to start work on Sunday, that's when I'd see if it had been worth the change.

Sunday morning came, I got to work by 8 o'clock to find most of the men already there, I called them together and explained what was expected of them, more smart remarks as usual but they were soon ready and got the job under way. A lot of credit for the job that day went to Dennis who was a born organiser and sorted out the casuals (casual labourers). It's so easy for individuals to 'prove' a method is wrong if they want to. But I told Dennis what my motives were and seeing the advantages he went at the job with a vengeance. By four o'clock it was all finished, tools cleaned, and everything away, I was well satisfied, and my own blokes had mucked in as well because they'd had the time to. All I'd done really was eliminated the time wasted waiting for each other, most of the time was usefully employed now. Next week we'd do 350 turfs in less time and with a lot less effort.

The following Saturday morning and having seen how much damage had been done the previous night I said that we wouldn't mess about we would take out the whole second bend. If the Sunday gang couldn't cope we'd still have Monday to finish it off before the evening meeting.

All day Saturday was spent preparing for Sundays turfing and still left time to do minor repairs. When we were loading the turves to be left ready for the morning we discovered that some outside contractors were digging a ruddy great trench across the nursery road, six foot deep and three foot wide. But we got what we wanted lifted and loaded and the contractor assured us it wouldn't actually be concreted yet. I wasn't worried too much because although the trench effectively cut off lorry access to the nursery I wasn't going to need any more until the following weekend and it was bound to be finished by then, wasn't it?

Sunday morning brought a change in the weather (just kidding), it was still raining, it was a lot heavier, and it was blowing the other way, it seemed to stop for a brief moment, so it was just the intensity and direction that altered.

As I was getting everybody organised someone announced the arrival of two lorries with a delivery of 2000 turf on each one and they were making their way toward the nursery.

How nice I thought, just what we need I don't think, but they had to be unloaded and that would alter all our plans. This sort of thing was going to happen often enough, if the new system couldn't cope with it, the system was no good.

I told one of the lads to tell the first lorry driver that we would have to find some steel plate to get over the trench as it had only been filled in with ballast and as it had rained all night long it would be a useless bridge. Unfortunately, he wasn't quick enough because the driver who was as familiar with the routine as anyone, hadn't realised that the muddy strip of soil was actually covering a deep trench and had driven straight across, sinking the back wheels deep into the loosely filled hole. Heaven knows how he didn't break an axle. 2,000 wet turves are a terrific weight and he'd gone right in lifting the nose of the truck, front wheels and all into the air. This was just the sort of delay I didn't need. Never mind, we would unload it where it lay and get some of the weight off, then maybe we could get the lorry (not to mention the driver) out of the hole.

Normally we would have used our forklift to unload the lorries but at that angle it was out of the question, anyway the blooming thing was out of action again. If you've never handled turf in the pouring rain you have never lived. One or two of the 'chaps' on realising what we were in for made a vain attempt to vanish, but they weren't allowed to. The lorry was unloaded turf by soggy turf and by the time the truck was empty there was mud all over the ground and us despite our weather-proof gear. We were a sorry sight, and it was no place for delicate ears, the crew thought of a new swear word for each of the sods moved, I even learned and used a few new ones myself.

One of the lads went off to get the heavy tractor to pull the truck out and after much pulling and pushing by men and machine, along with expert advice from all quarters, 'the committee' agreed it was not going to work. Then the tractor driver had a brainwave and disappeared towards the half-finished conference centre muttering something about a J.C.B being used there. Sure enough, before very long he was back followed by one those huge diggers complete with a willing driver. The Irish lad who drove it summed the scene up at a glance and almost without stopping he drove up behind the lorry and edged the bucket under it. As the back of the truck came up level with the road the J.C.B. moved forward across the ditch and gently lowered it to the ground. A big cheer went up especially from the lorry driver when he found that no real damage had been done. Having thanked the tractor driver, I yelled at my blokes that we still had a day's work to be finished and we now only had the afternoon to do it in, so let's get on with it.

We made our way back into the stadium to start a job three hours later than intended. Everybody got stuck into the task, got the blooming stuff down as best they could and hoped that conditions would be good enough on Monday to allow us to finish off.

Monday morning the weather had changed yet again and for once this time it was for the better. I couldn't believe that the rain had become a fine drizzle and there wasn't much coming down on my pitch, which allowed the respite needed to finish properly. I'd seen enough of the job to add another twist to the scheme and make a proposal to the chief engineer. So I went up to see him, a chap named Joe Dakin who has since gone on to bigger and better things, but he was a person who would listen to an argument and act on it, for or against. The key to my new method was to give an incentive to the blokes for using their time more effectively, it seemed obvious to the management but just because the stadium was to gain by improving the job, the benefits may elude the 'workers'.

The motivator was a tried and tested idea knows to me as 'job and finish', it meant just that, do the job and your day ends when the job was done. I would set the target, which in this case, was that they lay the turf, water and roll it, clean the tools, put them away and push off home. Joe Dakin eventually agreed and got the blessing from the General Manager, we would try it the following weekend. On Sunday I outlined the scheme to the 'super seven' it could only apply to the casuals; my own staff were hourly paid and would complete a full day anyway. Fortunately, they were a good bunch and there was an element of job satisfaction to encourage them along.

The area that we had prepared for them would take 350 turves, if they could do that in reasonable time I'd be well satisfied. They did and it was a first-class job, the area was turfed, rolled, a better clean up than usual, tools away and then they went home at 3.30 pm.

They were delighted and each subsequent performance, we increased the amount of turf laid, made better use of the time saved and everyone gained a little. But it came to an end sooner than I imagined when a sweeping ban on all overtime and so-called excess spending was imposed.

I have been around long enough to accept change in difficult times, but the effect of the sweeping cutbacks was soon seen in the gradual deterioration of the track and many other parts of the stadium. Eventually conditions weighted on the side of those who were advocating a change from grass to sand for the greyhound track. I don't know the benefit's in racing for or against sand, I don't know the first thing about greyhounds, but I do believe that powerful voices of bean-counters in high places aren't always qualified to see when they are getting value for money, they don't seem to connect a punter from a balance sheet.

Meanwhile Wembley has a sand track for the greyhound

racing which was gradually being transferred to my pitch and my office a shoe full at a time, and on the big match days when all and sundry have their 'walkabout' on our carefully prepared pitch, I could cry to see sandy footprints everywhere. Then you get the same people saying the pitch is in a bit of a state, that 'they are patching it up with sand'.

Never mind, when the dog racing followers finally disappear I'll concrete the track, paint it green and use it as a footpath, cost effective but will anyone pay to look at it?

© Ecophoto | Dreamstime.com

The dogs tear up the turf really badly on the bends

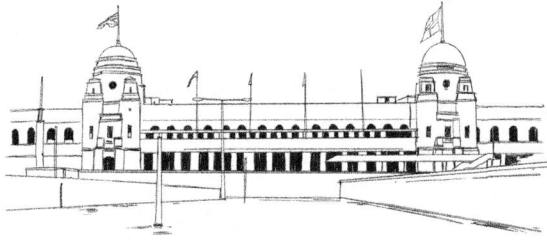

Chapter 6

Royalty, Rock Stars and Right Hon's

Over a period of time Wembley must see more than its share of VIPs, dating back to the official opening in 1924 by His Majesty King George V and even during my time, I have stood at the Royal Tunnel when a member of the Royal family has presided at a Wembley event. Usually this is in their role as guest of honour, meeting players and officials at the outset and presenting the medals and trophy at the end.

The most outstanding royal events in my mind are the Military Musical Pageants, my first being in 1977, the Jubilee year. At the heart of these writings, I make a lot of keeping people off of the pitch and even when teams are being presented to a VIP on the pitch, we roll out carpets. But for the Military Musical Pageant on that occasion and as a prelude to the main event, the Queen and HRH Prince Phillip drove through the ranks of reservists and volunteers from the three-armed services in a horse drawn landau. This was followed by four regiments of guard's bands, the combined bands of the household cavalry (more horses) and in all over 2,000 booted bandsmen played on that pitch for us that night. Absolutely fantastic and what they might have done to the sacred turf didn't enter into my mind. I just tapped along to the music and the occasion, thrilled with every minute.

I believe that there were about 50,000 spectators that evening, there usually is and this included a few thousand loyal subjects who were somewhat disappointed because the royal carriage didn't drive along the south side of the stadium, and I know because that was where the stadium staff and their families were seated. In fact, anybody with a complementary ticket, but I don't think this oversight was deliberate. Those folk cheered their Queen from a distance and had got much closer to their sovereign than most would in a lifetime.

The Princess of Wales didn't attend very often during my time, but the Queen Mum did. It always seems to be pouring with rain when she is at Wembley, I recall the day the Queen Mother went onto the pitch to shake hands with the team and turned down the offer of an umbrella. Her glare at the Wembley security officer was enough to make him step back. He said afterwards that it was because she did not want to be the only one undercover. However, I was pleased to see her accept the same officer's offer at a later visit when the heavens opened up. As fit as she was in many ways, no-one can afford to get wet and then sit in the royal box, even a heated one, not at her age, not at any age.

Wembley presentations are like the changing of the guard. Everything is done to the minute. The Royal Party or Guests of Honours Party, do not leave the tunnel until they are beckoned by an official on the Wembley staff, who would have already signalled the Players Tunnel for the two teams, led by their respective managers, to walk out and line up each side of the halfway line. The Chief Guest is usually accompanied by FA officials and In the case of an International Match, the Heads of the Foreign Football

Associations, or Directors of both clubs with domestic games. The Arena Marshall never takes his eye off his watch because that whistle will blow at three o'clock (or whatever the kick-off time is) regardless of anything that might happen. The captain of the first team is introduced to the guest and then that Captain in turn introduces each player. The Manager is presented last and then crosses over to the other side, finishing up with the referee and his officials. For school events and Rugby League Finals, the person that leads the community singing is also in that line up. Each person takes a couple of minutes and it usually runs to time. But not always! Princess Alexandra, a blue blooded royal if ever there was one, but also a mum was being presented to the players at a Rugby League Final and decided to enquire about the new baby born to the wife of one of them that very morning and in doing so nearly ruined the meticulous plans.

Princess Anne was guest of honour on a number of occasions that I was on duty and I got the impression that the Royals who spent most time at Wembley were the Duke and Duchess of Kent, both are very popular. The Duke of course was the president of the Football Association and played a very active part. You never see the Kent's look anything other than engrossed in whatever is happening on the field of play. Some VIPs show clearly on their faces that they would rather be somewhere else, anywhere else. Presumably if you have seen one you have seen them all. They must dread extra time.

Prince Michael of Kent and the Duke of Gloucester have attended although I can't recall too many visits. Then of course you get the Earl of Marlborough and one or two nobilities on the odd visit. Next, I suppose are the prime Ministers, my first was Harold Wilson. It was the wettest night I could remember.

Extra carpets were run out on the pitch so that Mr Wilson did not have to walk in the mud (had it been a year later it couldn't have happened when we drained the wings of the pitch). I'm sure the players stepped back a pace because when the prime minister stepped forward to shake hands with each player he had to step off the mat to reach them and got to the last one with soaking feet.

I saw Jim Callaghan at Wembley a number of times and could not pick out any particular event when he was Prime Minister. Whereas Mrs Thatcher I remember very clearly how on one occasion she seriously altered the routine sending the planners into a state of panic.

The routine on such occasions, is that all Guests of Honour are driven up through the Royal Tunnel, where they get out and walk up a few stairs to the 'The Royal Retiring room, but not that day. When 'Maggie' arrived a little early she realised, presumably, that a match was already in progress. It was 'only' the schoolboys six-a-side final being played, before the big event. She didn't go up to the Royal Retiring room as directed, but walked up the tunnel into the arena, looked around and found somewhere to sit on one of the benches used by players and officials of both teams. But because it wasn't the main match being played it was the odd teacher and ground staff, including myself, who were sitting there. In fact one of the lads, said to me "Doesn't that lady look like the Prime Minister". I think someone suggested she was probably an official from the English Schools Association. Then realisation of who it was hit me and others like a brick, it might have been the rather stressed looking officials supposedly looking after her but clearly uncomfortable. They looked lost for a minute, but she calmly told them she was alright and remained to see the end of the youngsters six-a-side.

It had been planned for Peter Purvis (BBC Blue Peter presenter) to present trophies to all the boys in the six-a-side semi-finals and finals. But he had obviously spotted her and calmly asked the PM if she would honour them and do the presentation in his place. She obliged to a very big cheer and my admiration, then with a wave to the crowd Mrs Thatcher went up to the Royal Box to do what she had come to Wembley to do, a very interesting lady.

People often think of the guest of honour as Royals or least dignataries, but we have had ex-footballers, sporting celebrities and others. I have spoken to a number of ex-players on Christian name level but at a big match I treated them as I would the Queen. One time a club manager and Sir Walter Winterbottom was talking with me about the pitch at a sports council meeting. I knew them both personally and naturally we used Christian names. Not long after that meeting Sir Walter was the guest of honour at a Cup Final, a stadium manager quietly reminded me to keep my staff and myself at a distance from the dignitaries, as if we needed to be told. We obviously accepted the situation but I did wonder why the FA didn't consider it appropriate for the Head Groundsman to line up and meet the Queen or the Chief Guest of the day. After all, his work is far more important than the disc jockey leading the singing and it's done at big cricket matches and definitely at Wimbledon. Sound like sour-grapes? Absolutely.

I have seen a number of Pop Shows at Wembley. I tend to be immersed in the preparation and skip the performance and still can't understand why the audience have to go on the pitch when normally 80-100,000 spectators can watch a Cup Final perfectly well from the terraces. No, they have to put 50,000 of 70,000 attendees on my ruddy pitch. Would the fans still hear all right? Well, they should be able to, most concerts can be heard all over Wembley, the town not the stadium. Yes of course I know that it's about the atmosphere and being close to their idols and waving candles, but thousands of pounds are spent making good the damage done by the fans after every show. Sour grapes? Absolutely.

You may have guessed that I am not a lover of pop music. As it happens I think some of it is really great music and my family let me know what is current, whether I like it or not. But my opinion doesn't affect my judgement when it comes to the pitch. I do have a lot of admiration for some of the pop stars. Elton John performed sell out concerts a number of times at Wembley but my memory of him is as Chairman of Watford FC and they had reached the FA Cup final in 1984. For obvious reasons Elton John wasn't just your run-of-the mill football club chairman and on the day he totally confused the management as he changed their whole procedure. He was on the pitch with the players from both teams before the match. He shook hands with anybody and seemingly everybody. He grabbed my hand so many times I thought he was going to propose. Tears of joy ran down his face, it seemed that he could not get over the fact he and his team were on the famous pitch at Wembley. He has done so much for Watford, and he is the type of chairman that has put millions into the club and from what I gather still allowed his very capable manager Graham Taylor, to manage. They were certainly a force to be reckoned with having come up from the fourth division in successive years but sadly for them Everton really outclassed Watford on the day but for all the best of reasons, the atmosphere was way above standard.

When it was over, Elton John once again came down to the pitch to console the players and both lots of fans gave him a terrific cheer. I heard mutterings from officials because the Watford chairman had broken with tradition, they would have liked him to go straight to the Royal Box and the reception afterwards. That day at Wembley stadium Elton John was the superstar in my book because he was so natural, tears and all, wouldn't it be nice if we could see some of the old fogies down on the pitch, showing a bit of passion? No, perhaps not.

Occasionally pop stars come to the ground, not necessarily to perform, sometimes to have publicity pictures taken, one was David Essex and a very nice lad he is. He came out dressed in the England football kit and I stood with him for a photo. This pleased me because I knew that my youngest daughter Linda was a big fan of David, so I planned to take a photo home framed and place it in her bedroom as a surprise. I got home from work that night determined not to say a word, but she rushed up to me and asked if I had got his autograph. I was shocked, how did she know, apparently everyone knew. It turned out that my wife had phoned the stadium earlier to speak to me and Arthur Rose (stadium foreman) took the call and told her that "Don is busy in a photo session with David Essex". Needless to say, when her mum told her, Linda got 'quite excited' and wanted her to phone again to make sure that I got his autograph, but she wouldn't, but I got it anyway. So much for my surprise!

I rubbed shoulders with a lot of the musical artists as they came in to look at the set up for their concert and occasionally got the impression that they were impressed with the size of the place from their perspective. One or two kicked a ball about, one or two looked quite useful.

I made a point of speaking to Pete Townsend of the rock band The Who. Even I knew how famous they were but that is all I knew but I also knew that he once lived next door to my wife when he was a teenager in Camden Town. Not surprisingly he was more interested in the stadium than obscure connections with my relatives. Quite a few of the groups speak to you, others got right up my nose, although to be fair, that was often as much to do with the entourage. The American stars seemed interested in Wembley as an interesting arena, the British often commented and were sometimes excited at performing in the 'home of football'.

Live Aid at Wembley was a marvellous achievement, and few could have guessed at the phenomena that it became and what it achieved. I was involved with the build-up and preparation as usual and the family kept me up to date as they enjoyed it on the TV, which is where I saw it from between doing something more interesting. All I could see on the day was a lot of work to be done from the next day onward, but what would I know?

As a concert arena, in my day, Wembley Stadium far exceeds any venue in the UK, capable of holding audiences of up to 100,000. But not without lorry loads of technical equipment to create a stage, sound systems and a pitch covered in boarding and tarpaulins, and even more equipment. The technical experts are amazing and the lorries and crew, clear the gear away, almost as fast as the crowds leave the arena. The boards, sheeting and the garbage, takes a little longer. There is an awful lot of rubbish left behind and I don't mean just empty cans and sweet wrappers.

Other show-business people, come to Wembley for a variety of reasons including Eric Morecambe, who was going to do a piece for TV, about the approaching Cup Final with Elton John. Eric was going to play the role of head groundsman and Elton John would be his assistant. Brian Moore and Dicky Davies from ITV were to come onto the pitch and interview the head groundsman (Eric), but true to his character (probably mine too) he told them to push off as they were a week too late, followed by a cross chat between them. I didn't hear it myself but I was told it was very funny. Unlike many others, Eric Morecambe didn't leave at once, he stayed to sign autographs and posed for photos with a load of youngsters. He even took the time to show one lad how to use his own camera. I went into a large group of these boys to ask Eric for his autograph. He looked at me and said, 'My what a big lad, what school do you come from sonny?' Can you imagine, I was eighteen stone, six feet tall and white hair, but when someone told him I was the groundsman, he went serious and we discussed the pitch, lawns and gardens etc. A very funny man, a real star and not too opinionated to talk,

Windsor Davies was like that too. He came to the Rugby League Finals to take community singing, on the first time with Don Estelle, the second with Mervin Hayes. All three starring in the TV comedy 'It Ain't Half Hot Mum'. They stood in the Royal Tunnel awaiting their cue but also chatting to the ground staff. Not to the upper crust who would so dearly love to be seen with the VIPs, after all these show-business folk are just doing their job, the same as my staff were doing.

When I was at school I remember pretending to be a cowboy or soldier and acting those parts with great conviction. The only difference was we made the script up as we went along. For a school play, I played Anthony in Julius Caesar and what is more I did the Brutus part as well. Although just a schoolboy, apparently I convinced the audience that I was Anthony, more important I convinced myself. I know it isn't that simple but actors or any other show- business folk are usually just people first and become something else when called upon, at least that has been my experience.

Some years ago, Bill Maynard came to Wembley with other

well-known actors to shoot scenes for a series called 'Trinity Tales', based upon 'The Canterbury Tales'. It was about a party of odd bods travelling to Wembley Stadium for the Rugby League Cup Final. I recall the producer Tristan DeVere Cole, a very tall man who told me I looked very much like Bill Maynard; then wanted me to meet the star of the show. At the time there may have been a resemblance and as Bill Maynard went to shake hands, I said to him " I am told you are to be my stand in." Fortunately, he thought it amusing and it proved to me he was not a stuffy bloke like so many personalities. Mind you, I am convinced the real stars are the most natural people 'no side' as they say. The jumped-up type can be a pain in the bum. I have seen film extras who do a couple of lines on commercials strutting around and talking as though they are Sir John Gielgud, Sir Ralph Richardson and Lord Olivier rolled into one. We've had plenty of those at Wembley usually shooting a commercial and I have seen better acting from one of my staff, when he comes in late telling a story to make you cry.

Getting back to the Trinity Tales. On the last day of shooting the director thought it would be a good idea to have the real groundsman and staff in the player's tunnel to make it more authentic. It was Boxing Night when the last scene with me and my gang was to be broadcast, so I insisted we watched it, the rest of the family wanted another channel. When it came to the end of the show, as the players ran out of the tunnel, we were nowhere to be seen, not one of us. We can only assume that the union objected to us being in the film or just cut. My family were not pleased with me I can tell you. I was called a lying so-and-so and a bloody nuisance because they had missed a good programme on the other side. We had no video then.

Another TV drama partly filmed at Wembley was 'Quatermass',

a science fiction drama and even regular visitors would never have recognised the stadium by the time the set people had finished with it. All sorts of weird paintings covered the concrete. Ornate graphics plastered all over the walls and the Twin Towers and the main pedway (Pedestrian Road from Olympic Way) was decorated in some very queer signs and I swear the whole thing was only seen for minutes when screened. Sometimes film and TV companies are there for days but if you go to the toilet when it's broadcast you might miss Wembley's part in the picture. I used to get annoyed when producers demanded the stoppage of mowers and tractors in fact anything noisy and as I've mentioned, everything in the empty stadium is noisy. As I understand it, the Stadium were paid, but sometimes the ground staff were held up for two and three hours a day, leaving the lads having to rush around to finish their normal work after filming. For example, the ground staff may get just a few minutes notice to put one or both goals up, including nets, which can often prove to be a blooming nuisance, especially when marking out or spraying or spreading chemicals.

Using Wembley Stadium for documentary films are also understandable, I guess that there have been dozens made related to the Olympics, Rugby League as well as soccer of course and the television and news reel archives are full of fascinating material to support them.

A particularly interesting documentary team was from a German TV company that came to Wembley to make a film about Helmut Schön, who was due to retire as the very successful manager of West Germany. Most of the German TV crew spoke excellent English so communication was no problem, until it got heated, at which point understanding appeared to be one way only.

In fact, they were very insistent when they arrived demanding the necessity for a goal with nets, unfortunately the instructions I had received said that nets would not be required, so I was not about to jump to attention willingly and someone had stormed off to talk to the 'management'. At which point a charming lady who had up to then been at the periphery of the film crew, came over to me and I freely admit, used her considerable charms to request that we put nets up when loud demands had failed. I explained that I was not being awkward, I had expected them to be at the stadium for a couple of days only and we had plenty of work to be getting on with. Despite which this very charming women (a producer I think) was still worrying me to put the nets up. So I explained again to her and 'management' that had appeared out of their offices, that it was Wednesday afternoon, and we were getting ready for a Rugby Final to be played on Saturday. I had a casual crew coming in at 6pm on Thursday to put the rugby posts up, which meant the pitch had to be measured and marked out during the day on Thursday, therefore we couldn't have a complete set of football posts in the way. Their seemingly simple request was clearly going to impact on that schedule, and it was becoming a serious problem.

My deputy (Jacky) who would take the brunt of the work and had taken an instant dislike to this film crew anyway, was meanwhile doing his best to talk me out of agreeing to nets. In fact he said 'quote' "do what you ******* like, but mark my words that lady would probably sleep with you to get the nets put up" (or words to that effect).

I offered my apology on his behalf, it was uncalled for and even allowing for his bitterness towards the German nation for whatever reason, I considered it well over the top. The lady who had obviously heard the remark, smiled at me and said nothing, but I was probably embarrassed and not a little bit cross with

Jacky. The next day the first thing my deputy saw when he arrived was that we had put the nets up after he had gone home and not surprisingly, he was fuming. As he approached the film crew who were also early, our delightful lady producer called out to my colleague "As you can see, the nets have been put up, but I had to pay your price, it was a good idea though, thanks". And turned away. She was joking of course, but my little mate was never too sure how she had got me to put the nets up, he probably thought bribery in other ways so when the story was relayed to me later, I said that "I couldn't possibly comment".

But then it was Thursday and the filming had gone on for a fourth day, I started to measure and mark out the Rugby League pitch but by 7pm we had rugby posts at one end and still the German crew were in the way at the other. I pleaded and begged and threatened. We were behind schedule, and I finally forced them off the pitch by erecting the soccer post in front of the rugby posts. They admitted defeat and we took the posts down and cleaned up the lines. We parted good friends; I posed for photos with 'The Cap' (Helmut Schön) but I am sad to say that I never saw the documentary or the photos.

We had kidded Jacky about the price that they had seemingly paid for the nets, but the real joke was on me because she was a very beautiful woman. If only I had been famous, good looking, talented or just less gullible. So much for telling someone to get off of my pitch!

For the annual Women's Hockey International, in 1981, England versus Wales, Her Majesty the Queen Elizabeth presided, to the absolute joy of her cheering, screaming, mainly schoolgirl subjects. Her Majesty was driven around the greyhound track in a special open top Range Rover, to the applause of nearly 70,000 banner waving, noisy spectators. Which continued throughout the game, somehow managing to blot out all other sound. Including, I understand, the whistle of the umpire, who had to be supported by officials on the touchline sounding a klaxon. There is no other 'Wembley Roar' like it, perhaps it's the higher pitch of young females, as different to the usual mainly older males, and they don't let up. The crowd attending the Hockey International match every year, creates a sound of its very own, its continuous and great fun.

On that occasion an over-zealous stadium engineer, making what I assumed to have been a last-minute inspection, ordered all the spare staff to stand in front of a tractor that was parked in the brake yard tunnel. The reason given was to hide it, in case, the Queen saw this 'untidy' piece of equipment. I can just imagine Her Majesty going home to Buck house and saying, 'It was a disgrace, so untidy, they even left a tractor where it could be seen'. I seem to remember seeing images of the Queen, driving a tractor and presumably there are a few dotted about the various royal estates, so she probably knows what they look like.

The most outstanding Royal events to my mind are the Military Musical Pageants.

The wonderfully noisy schoolgirl spectators for the
Womens Hockey International March 1981

© by kind permission of The Hockey Museum. Photographer Pat Ward.

Her Majesty Queen Elizabeth II, seen here being driven
around the Wembley pitch at the Womens Hockey
International, England v Wales March 1981

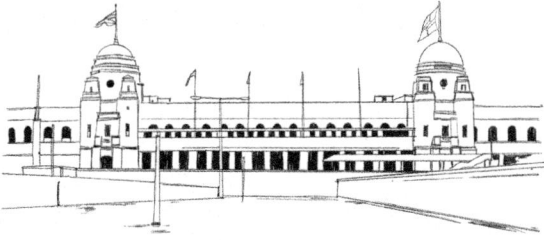

Chapter 7

Speedway Tracks, Who Needs Them?

Did you know about the speedway track? We had one at the Empire Stadium Wembley, and except for the thousands of speedway fans, I bet most regular spectators didn't know before I mentioned it earlier. Probably never seen it when you have been to a match or watched a final on the TV? Well, that's not so surprising, it's kept mostly under the surface so to speak, but ready to come out once or twice every few years, so it had to come up sometime on my watch. As you know Wembley stages different events, almost any event that has a need to accommodate thousands of spectators even if it means we have to lift up some of the sacred turf to make it fit. You see, the inside perimeter of an international speedway track comes well inside that of the size of a football or rugby pitch; subsequently we have to lift the turf along one side each time it's held there. The World Speedway Championship had been held at Wembley since 1936 and with the exception of WW2 years, almost continuously until the 60's, when it shared the load with other countries, then in 1975 it was my turn to take it on.

It wasn't too bad actually, because it was done using the same method that the ground staff had used for donkeys' years. e.g. Take up the appropriate amount of turf, remove the soil and replace it with shale. Easy! I'll tell you how it's done in case you are ever asked to do one yourself.

About a week before the 'heavy work' contractors were due to arrive, a couple of the ground staff string out the perimeter of the inner track, in other words they use range lines and pins to lay out the exact shape of the inside edge of where the speedway track will be. The bends, the shaped ends are already there, you would have seen them lots of times. What, you thought it was just a nice design?

Take a closer look next time; they are the 'D' shaped sand pits behind each goal. Then, using turfing irons or 'half-moons' as some people call them they cut the turf following the lines around. When the contractors arrive with their turf cutting machine, they will cut out uniform size turfs following the line of the cut precisely. These are then palletised so that a forklift may take them to the 'nurseries', where they are re-laid as carefully as if we were creating a mini-Wembley pitch. Whilst there the turf will be watered, cut and cared for in exactly the same way as it would were they inside the stadium. We have to, we will want them back soon and it will have to match perfectly, this is not the place for a patchwork quilt.

Next! All the soil left behind has to be removed and again stored where we can get it later, leaving a layer of compressed ash. In 1975 the ash was to stay there, as it had for the previous forty years, but it gave me a chance to look at what I was going to be tackling when the next Championship Final was due to be held and when I planned to put in my drainage system.

Then, in come wagons of shale, tons and tons of the stuff and huge bulldozers to push it into place, smoothing and compressing it under the immense weight, although still not enough. We next bring in a grading machine, rather an old-fashioned thing but then some of us are, it's very effective all the same. It consists of a large blade attached to a frame on iron wheels, the idea of it being to scrape the surface lumps and bumps until it's smooth enough for the high-speed bikes to travel over. At the same time a lorry, heavily laden with even more shale, follows around adding its own weight to the job and supplying extra material for the pitted sections shown up by the grader. Are you still with me?

Whilst this goes on, the newly created surface is sprayed with water and every inch of the track is carefully examined for possibilities of subsidence or ridges, the life of a rider might depend on the extra attention to detail. Around this activity the heavy gang are putting the special fences up. These are chain link fencing pulled into place about 18' inside the greyhound track fence, they go right around the perimeter and act as a barrier to any stray bikes which may decide to hurtle toward the crowd.

As I watched this transformation for the first time, very much in awe and fascination, I was reminded of another Gallacher family tale about a similar fence built many years previously and meant to protect the spectators from speedway bikes. Unfortunately, it didn't stop a bike running my dad over, but then he was track side, not spectator side, which wouldn't have helped. Forgive the interruption.

Way back in 1928 our Dad, (Patrick, Joseph Gallacher) was the head groundsman at the original West Ham Stadium, a vast arena so big it wasn't necessary to lift parts of the football pitch to lay down a speedway track, that track went around a pitch and just to rub it in, the greyhound track went around that. It was opened in the 20's, naturally enough to make money, but not out of football but greyhounds and speedway, which were apparently even more popular. It was a tremendous place, capable of holding 120,000 fans. Anyway, it was the morning of a big speedway meeting and father was busy checking safety fencing and had no reason not to feel perfectly safe, particularly as it was at a time of day when riders weren't allowed on the track even to practice. It was and is still, a very well organised sport. However, life is full of surprises and as they say, there is always one isn't there?

Well, there was certainly 'one' on this fateful morning. It seems that an amateur rider not only ignorant of the rules regarding when he could practice, but also those related to the direction he should ride around a track. You would have thought that was fairly basic information but clearly a mystery to this particular rider, who may well have had steamed up goggles too, something we will never know. Anyway, according to the family story, the speedway rider had gone out on the track for a quick practice. My Dad, alerted to the sudden roar of a powerful bike in what had been a deathly silent arena looked up and toward what should have been the direction a bike would have appeared. Unfortunately, this wayward rider came at him around the bend at high speed in a clockwise direction not the direction that the entire speedway world except this character rode, anti-clockwise. Experts at the time suggested that that fact may have accounted for him going completely out of control. That and hitting my old man in the rear, slamming Dad, bike and rider into the fence. Track marshals and stewards rushed to the scene to pull the bike and bodies apart. My older brother Eddie was on the ground staff at the time, and he was one of the first to get to them and it must have been a heck of a shock, not just seeing the accident but realising that one of the victims was his Dad. But according to Eddie, the blood soaked and very still figure was barely given a second look, the impact had been too much to survive, there was obviously no question that Father might be alive, so someone threw an old sack over the body.

Later as the story was told and retold few could agree whether it had been Father's physique (he was a big bloke), the high content of brown-ale (a rumour) or just pig headedness (probably), that enabled him to beat the odds for surviving. But one observant helper saw the 'corpse' move, a closer examination found that he was in fact still breathing so an ambulance was called, and he was rushed to hospital. At the Seaman's Hospital not too far away, the doctors pronounced his survival nothing short of a miracle. His head was badly lacerated, hence the tremendous amount of blood, he had broken ribs and cuts and bruises covered his body from top to toe. I don't remember being told how long it took for dad to recover or how the rider fared, but when the first bike powered up at the Wembley track I made sure I was well out of the way. I didn't fancy a nose-to-nose confrontation with one of those machines, I might not have come off as well as Father did.

So, back to building a speedway track. Just in front of the player's tunnel, the gang built a big double gate into the fence, this enabled the riders to come on and off the track in the safest way and the tunnel also doubled up as the 'pit's'. If you are one of the many thousands of fans that follow speedway, this tunnel is just the spot to soak up the atmosphere. The smell of high-octane fuel and burnt exhaust plus the tremendous noise from high powered machines revving away will make the enthusiast get downright excited. Me, I can't stand the smell or the noise, my brother Eddie would have loved it, whereas I never have been a motorbike fan so

71

I kept well away and left that stuff to the aficionados.

At the Royal tunnel they created a 'starting gate', quite a complicated affair really, they have a square of turf cut out exposing a socket for the gate to hang on and cables are wired through it. A long line of flags is erected parallel to the home straight and extra lighting put in, we put a tractor on the sand at the East end of the pitch and we're nearly ready. It's starting to look like a speedway track now. The tractor by the way, is an ancient old beast but did a very useful job at those meetings. Attached to the back is a gate grader and between each race the tractor makes a complete circuit, levelling out the churned-up surface, smoothing out the ruts and furrows created by the racing bikes. All that was needed to complete the scene are the 'rakers', a team of men on each bend where the worst damage occurs and where they patch up what the grader doesn't. That's it, it's ready.

Thursday is Trials Day, Saturday is the night of the big meeting, Sunday? Then on Sunday we take the ruddy lot up again. Away go the flags, lights and gates. Down comes the safety fencing, dig up the shale, bring back the soil, go and get the turf from the nursery and don't break any of it. Get the turf laid, fill in the gaps and see if we can't make this place look as though it's got a football pitch. No more speedway for another year. Mother is it worth it?

Well apparently, for the World Speedway Championship Final, the gate always exceeds 80,000. Champions are created, speedway fans get a thrill out of every minute and don't feel the need to climb over the barriers or wreck the place to express their joy. They manage to demonstrate that in other ways, so as far as I am concerned they can come back as often as they like, even if my pitch does get the edges lifted like a blooming doormat.

By the time that the '78 Championship Final came around I was ready and willing to lift the edges, it was an ideal opportunity to lay down my drainage system just where it was desperately needed. This time when the surface shale was taken out, we went deeper, digging out some ancient black cinders – this stuff must have been there when the Olympics were held and in hindsight, we should have put it in jars and sold it off as mementos, but it looked too horrible to keep. On the day I did wonder where it was going because you're not allowed to dump stuff just anywhere. Typically, when you've got it, nobody wants it, when you finally find somewhere to put it, all you see are adverts for 'hardcore' wanted. Anyway, someone thought of the ideal place, on the site where they held a Sunday Market. The area wasn't concrete in those days so if anything, it helped and it was right outside our door.

When we reached the correct depth we put in a layer of washed clinker about a foot deep, then we laid the drains down, the same type that was under the rest of the pitch. The pipes lay laterally, with a fall toward the half-way line. At that point they picked up the main drainage pipe which ran under the full width of the pitch, with outlets well away from the turf. When the fall was correct, another layer of washed clinker was pressed in on top of the pipe. It started off nearly two feet deep, but by the time we had finished it was less than half that.

What's next? Oh yes, next .....this is starting to sound like a cookery lesson, isn't it, sorry about that, bear with me it's almost done. Next, we add about four inches of shingle which in turn is covered in sharp sand, again its spread very evenly; this combination is what will stop the compost being washed down through the larger material below. 'What compost'? I'm getting to

73

that. Right, next comes the compost, peat soil and sand. We grade this of course, level it out using rakes quite a lot and our feet a lot more, never a roller. If there is a bump or a hole, treading every inch will pass the message up to your brain, a roller can't do that yet. So as your feet find each dip or rise you can fill in or scrape away as necessary. Then, when it's thoroughly trodden in, even out the soil to the level that you want with the back of a big rake, and you will have the perfect surface on which to lay the turf.

Now put down your pencils and I'll tell you what we achieved by this stolen opportunity in 1978. Never mind the speedway track. We created a playing surface that would no longer trap water two inches below the surface on top of a load of compressed clinker, for one complete wing of the famous pitch. At last, the rain would pass through the turf and the compost layers allowing the drainage system to do its job. For years and years, the wings had been a disgrace, left to the vagaries of the weather. But then it only showed up when it rained! Now if it was subjected to a deluge, the effect on the whole pitch was consistent. If it was wet on the wing it was the same wet in the middle the corners or the penalty areas. Not just the bit which almost annually we ripped up to create a speedway track. The same applied visa-versa of course, in certain circumstances the offending sides could still be pretty wet whilst the rest of the surface was dry, regardless of our best efforts to even it out.

Unfortunately, just when I believed I had excelled myself, it wasn't quite finished. When the speedway racing was over and the turf laid, it looked marvellous and under test conditions, deliberately flooding it etc; everything passed muster. But less than a week later, after a particularly heavy downpour, a puddle of water formed on one of the corners. Nothing dramatic, but after all of my bragging, it wasn't going to be good enough. What had happened and you might care to make a note of this, the permanent ends of the track were now slightly higher than the level of the pitch. As a consequence, during any serious downpour the corner was getting more than its fair share. Therefore, it needed something extra, but what?

It was so difficult to simulate the extreme conditions needed to make it show up, it was after all a massive improvement and could easily have gone unnoticed, but not by me. A sense of pride said I, conceit or pig-headedness said others. So, for a while, whenever the heavens opened up I could be found out on the pitch or sitting up in the stands to watch what happened, looking out for the trouble spots. It wasn't that bad actually, the main surface cleared very quickly but the corners were draining too slowly for my liking and even though the area in question was behind the goal line and unlikely to affect play, it was in the 'drain chain' and a potential bottleneck under extreme conditions. Obviously the water wasn't getting away at the same rate, so we would have to give it a little help. My own ground staff got stuck in laying land drains right across the ends of the ground around the D's to improve the soak away under the sand. It worked all right but being a pessimistic sort of a devil and not wishing to leave anything to chance, I planned to improve it even further at the next opportunity. As you might imagine, there is little time to mess around with such activities in between the scheduled events and the next opportunity didn't arise until the following summer. As it turned out we didn't suffer from any water problems but then we hadn't experienced a period of continuous wet weather in that time either. So, I was still left with a bee in my bonnet about taking the drainage a stage further.

But by June 1978 the bulk of the work was completed, the

groundsman and his staff were actually referred to as miracle men during the TV commentary of the Ipswich v Arsenal FA Cup Final, praise which we gladly accepted. The media only turn up at the stadium for the big occasions which Is not as often as you might think, and as journalists tend to follow their particular sport, quite infrequent. So having been used to seeing the Wembley pitch a quagmire whenever it rained, and it had rained for a solid week before that match, the television pundit's, press and presumably the teams expected much of the same. They were a little surprised to find a pitch which actually lived up to the reputation that was finally deserved.

It hadn't stopped raining until an hour before the kick-off then the sun came out and by the time that the game was under way the surface wasn't even slippery. Despite the deluge the pitch was ruddy marvellous.

The final part of the drainage puzzle was put in place a year later and when the time came we dug trenches from the corner flags to the edge of the grass, each one some 28ft long, then along the ends around the sand and this time we built a SILT PIT under the sand at each end. These were connected to the outgoing drainage system with yet more land drains and after testing the areas by flooding them with hoses for many hours, I was finally satisfied. Well almost. I was still a bit concerned that with the enormous area of that stadium catching and channelling water down the same system that drained my pitch, I could have done with one more outlet. Still, that as the engineers commented, was going a bit far, or so I thought at the time, later on you will see what I mean.

I could see that I wouldn't have to worry about the pitch going back to those terrible conditions we experienced before, I had no intention of ever seeing again, the surface looking like the seashore after the tide had gone out. The best talent in the world look to Wembley as the Mecca of top sports, it's said to be among the most famous stadiums in the world. Now I've tried to give that talent the best playing surface too – so bring on the bikes, and sod the rain.

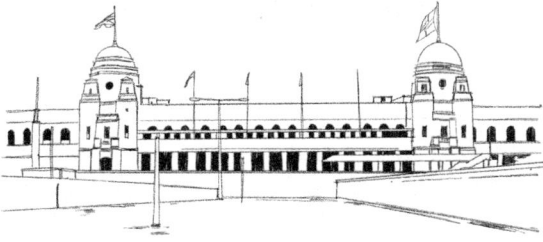

Chapter 8

It's a Bit of a Worry

'When I was young and in my prime' - that's how the saying starts, doesn't it? When I was younger and in my prime, I actually loved being a groundsman, working ridiculous hours in ludicrous conditions for little or no money and I did it because I actually enjoyed it.

If I were to make a list of the all the jobs I have done in my life it would be a hell of a long one, mostly manual, some managerial, always what most people would regard as hard labour, but I have never shied away from a day's work. From the furnaces of a North London steel mill to the freezing, back breaking Leicestershire coal mines and most building work in between. But whenever the opportunity arose, I kept going back to the sports grounds.

For a great many years, I worked on one such sports ground in North London, which was owned by a Jesuit college, although it was a few miles away from the college it was in effect their playing field. It happened to be the playing field that my father had worked on, which backed on to the street where I was born and so, with my brothers, I had grown up on it and could claim to know every blade of grass and bump in the ground.

There were many occasions when close friends, family, even people who barely knew me, suggested I get a 'proper' job with decent hours and wages and they may well have been right, but I didn't think so at the time.

A typical day's work on that ground started when it got light and ended after dark, and that's a long day in the summer and sometimes felt longer in the winter. It was rare that the ground wasn't used seven days each week, which meant that I was being used seven days every week. But that was typical of the fifties and sixties, not just with groundwork, but many trades worked at least six days a week for eight or nine hours a day and few holidays. The trouble was that such a workload, again like many trades, tends to carry a price later-on in life. I was constantly warned by better people than me, that I ought to take more care, but I was oblivious to all that, I was enjoying it. On that sports ground, apart from a short time when I had an assistant, who, poor old devil, could barely lift a box of matches to light his 'roll-ups' but was fine driving the tractor, in effect I was on my own. And because of the lack of help and the continuous struggle just to get supplies and materials, I was always 'making do' and finding ways of 'managing' the workload and responding to the increasing demands of my dozen or so 'bosses' mainly made up of college staff.

But that was all right, I was as fit as a fiddle and a bit of a big head so everything was just another way of 'proving' I could do things against the odds. I saw nothing strange or wrong about driving a tractor for hours in the pouring rain getting soaked through (no cab in those days). 'I don't suffer from colds' I would have said 'and anyway it's got to be finished by Monday.' Or whenever, there's always a good reason isn't there? I saw nothing unusual about having to push a lorry load of sand a barrow load at a time 200 yards from where it had been unloaded to where it had to go and spreading it with a shovel and rake; there was no other way; there was only me, no fuel for the tractor or no tractor and the pitch would have needed it. The ground always needed something. I knew I was straining myself every year when I raised the sixteen, forty-foot-high rugby posts on my own. Digging out the post holes, creating a barrier on one side of the hole, lifting the 'skinny' end above my head and walking up the pole until the 'thick' end guided its way into the hole and I could get it upright enough to jam wedges around the base with my feet. Sometimes, if I was lucky. I found a helper to put their foot on the base of the pole to guide it into the hole thereby saving me a couple of 'missed' attempts as it skidded across the hole while the top end bounced off of my shoulders. Then all I had to do was fasten the crossbars on my own, one end was manageable, the other end was a combination of ingenuity, brute force and ignorance. It should have been impossible for one person to do but in a perverse sort of way, I was proud of it. I didn't actually say so and I rarely had an audience other than my Alsatian dog anyway, but looking back, I was really very proud of it. My obvious naivety didn't allow for the fact that as long as the job got done like that, year on year, the boss (head master of the college) didn't actually have to do anything about getting me help, so he didn't.

For almost twenty years I did the job any way that brain and brawn knew how with the resources to hand. In the winter I created and maintained four rugby pitches for the benefit of 700 college boys playing most days for five days each week. Oh, and by the way, that muddy lot didn't look after the communal showers or clean out the pavilion after them, I did it. Then in the summer it was cricket and athletics which meant two good wickets and a

4-lane quarter mile running track, all on grass.

It wasn't a permanent cinder track, that was too easy, this was measured and marked each year and had to be rubbed out when it was finished with. When I think back to the time and effort it took marking then brushing out a mile or so of white lines, it makes me wonder why I didn't take another job the way I was advised. Oh, and on the college annual sports day they wanted a Royal Marine style assault course for the cadets which went around the outside of the playing field. Let me see now, a ten-foot wall of railway sleepers, rows of hanging tyres, canvas tunnels, jumps, a water filled trench and other paraphernalia that you might have seen on the television in a military tattoo but I saw in my sleep. Come to think of it, the railway sleepers were a lot worse to lug about than the rugby posts. No matter, the point being that I remember caring less about the physical effort. What got me down was getting the task completed to the satisfaction of differing instructions. For me, getting it right meant looking at the job in context but often the purpose was lost in the aspirations of some individuals among the teaching staff.

Groundwork anywhere has an overall problem involving the seasons of course and the ever-changing unpredictable weather and the wear and tear applied. Grass is a living thing, affected by what man does to it but not terribly cooperative. It's not like a stretch of tarmac road that can be patched up when it's wearing thin to bring it up to standard again. So my judgement on a job was based on skills that come from years of experience, guidance from my betters and indeed what I learned at my father's knee, including like so many of my peers, making do with what you had to hand.

Unfortunately, as any groundsman will tell you should you ask, when it comes to an opinion about driving, sport or politics, the man in the street is an expert with a view that's intractable. That's where the pressure comes in, because the same such people are just as vociferous about the quality of a playing surface, particularly a football pitch as in Wembley or a cricket table as in Lords, the Oval or one created for a bunch of second eleven college boys.

When I was employed by the college the experts were made up of every game master, form master and the head-master (mostly Jesuit priests), the headmaster's secretary, parents, and even the occasional college boy if he thought he was big enough. Everyone had an opinion, a multitude of chiefs and just one Indian, me!

The old adage of not letting the b......s grind you down are all very well, but when you have little or no redress and no-one but yourself to fight your corner, it's very difficult to beat. But I believed at the time that I did. Whether their wants or opinions were polite or aggressive, it was usually momentary, and they eventually went away leaving me to get on with it. Anyway, as long as the majority were satisfied, and I didn't cost the college any money, I generally shrugged it off and just concentrated on producing the results. By the way, did I mentioned that I lived in a 'tied' cottage, that may have affected my judgement somewhat.

At weekends in the summer, it was cricket for the 'Old Boys' (former college boys) and as any man who cares for a cricket table will tell you, most cricketers, especially those that claim to play for 'the love of the sport' know exactly what they want from a wicket, unfortunately it never seemed to be the one that you've just provided. The one that you have laboured to produce for them on the day and you thought was pretty good. Perish the thought that they were in the least bit fussy; after all it's an extremely amateur event for extremely amateurish cricketers.

"But Don, I would have expected that ….." and heaven help me if they had a bad result batting or bowling. I can still see images of batsman looking at the ground as though the shattered wicket had nothing to do with their lack of skill and everything to do with a worm cast. Some worm!

Just like all of my brothers, I played most sports at quite a serious level and particularly loved to play cricket and although I was not a college 'Old Boy', I did turn out for them for many years. A typical summer Sunday for me was to spend all the morning finishing off the wicket (probably still marking it and erecting the stumps as the players arrived). To dash indoors, change into whites, play cricket until tea, roll the wicket during the interval and bat or field when the others came out; and I loved every minute of it.

Now in the main, my teammates tempered any criticism of the wicket with 'light-hearted' humour, albeit with a bite because, after all, I hadn't turned up in a smart car and was still only the groundsman. I wasn't even an 'Old Boy'; I hadn't attended the sainted college. Whereas the visitors who had no such concern for my feelings, justified or not, voiced their opinion accordingly and that I remember did get to me. Although not that much, or so I believed, because after each match both teams would end up at the local for a 'pint' including me and eventually the visitors would go home, only to be seen twice each year. Not important you see, I directed my concerns at the job, not to catering to the whims of individuals. Or so I thought.

When I became groundsman at Hampstead Cricket Club the worries were much the same and although I was conscious that the much higher standards of cricket played there demanded the best of me, it didn't cause me any distress because I'd only ever given of my best whether the players had been schoolboys or, as most at

Hampstead were, County class cricketers. The biggest difference for me was in the working conditions and for once I wasn't stinted for the price of a bag of seed. The psychological effect of this up-market sports ground was only in my head. Now the critical 'experts' were few and far between, despite the fact that these men were blooming experts and had played on some of the best cricket grounds in the land and in my mind, fully entitled to say what they felt. But they didn't whine or moan or have tantrums in the way I had experienced before. When something about the wicket was causing concern it was invariably said through the captain or the club secretary and even then it was always in the manner of a 'discussion' not a demand or criticism. It was such a revelation and the time I was there was a very satisfying period of my working life.

It will be fairly obvious to the reader that this is something of a hobby horse of mine and at Wembley the voice of the critic is far reaching. But when the moaners say that the grass is too long or too short, or too wet or too dry, it may well be correct, but unless it's a pitch or a wicket that favours the home team who are used to any idiosyncrasies, why is it relevant? On a neutral ground such as Wembley, the odd conditions shouldn't favour one side or one individual. If the grass is sky blue, pink with lumps in it, it's exactly the same for everyone on the park. Surely that's one of the reasons they change ends in football or rugby, so whatever is the problem? In my view and to some extent, my experience, if you can play, you can play on any pitch in any conditions, the competition will be equally handicapped.

Go to the West Indies, Pakistan or South Africa and see where the greatest cricketers in the world learned their craft and still play matches on from time to time and I don't mean the test wickets, I mean the local schools, park or back street.

What about football? The greatest players of all time learned to play in alleyways or at best, mocked up pitches of baked clay, beaches or concrete. Not the pristine conditions demanded by those who are having a rough day and not living up to the images created by the press or their agent. If you think that's far-fetched consider the breeding grounds for the stars from Brazil, Argentina, Portugal, Spain or Italy. See conditions the Greek, Israeli or Korean players train on and before you dismiss them as third world, watch out, they reach World Cup qualifiers and through skills acquired on 'daft' pitches they often manage to give the 'super' nations a ruddy good run for their money. While I'm at it, it won't be long before African national teams emerge, the ones that I have seen are no mugs and what do you suppose they were playing on, bowling greens? Apart from the big clubs or the national side, I don't think so. That's where the next Pele, Jairzinho, Eusiebio will come from in the future (if you are not old enough to know the names, look them up) and what are the European superstars going to say to their manager when they play away – the sands too deep, the clay is too cracked? Think about it, some of the most exciting cup ties in recent years have been a lower division team at home on a decidedly dodgy pitch, against a club used to better conditions and sometimes those lowly mortals kill the giants.

Sorry about that, I do go off on one when there's no-one to stop me and clearly, I could bore you to death if I haven't already done so. Although you shouldn't be bored yet, presumably this is the first time you have read this, whereas I've heard me say it dozens of times.

Fortunately, in case you missed it, the example of my experience at Hampstead Cricket Club, would suggest that the better the standard of sportsman, the less likelihood there is of unqualified criticism and no-one, even me, should be worried about qualified, professional, constructive criticism. Therefore, it follows that going to Wembley Stadium, home of the major English Finals, where the best players in the world go to perform would indicate that I had cracked it, I shouldn't have to worry about petty unprofessional moaning should I? I shouldn't, should I?

Alas, the theory is flawed, somewhere between Hampstead and Wembley, just a few miles as the crow flies, I had picked up some 'experts' that had I rarely came across before. It's true that I talk to some of the most knowledgeable men or women in the world of sport, legendary team managers and even exchange tips with the occasional television personality about their aspirations for the lawn at home to look a bit like my pitch. But 'experts' whose main concern is to fill column inches and keep viewers occupied before, during and after a game are part of being in the topflight of my game and it can sometimes be a worry.

Now, if I said that the 'ultimate' source of any stress was the media it would seem ridiculous, but actually there is a lot of truth in it. Needless to say, I am not chased by paparazzi when I go 'clubbing', I doubt if an editor would know my name and hope he doesn't. But the 'experts' that I work for, the management, those in charge, care an awful lot what the media say, or even 'might' say about Wembley, rightly so and they of course will then tell me.

I might have mentioned earlier that I was interested in making the Wembley pitch a better playing surface. Whereas previously the main aim was for it to 'look' fantastic, which it did, and this 'look' was matched by the expectations of the media on behalf of the public; hence references to the 'sacred' turf etc; But the drive to be the best looking came at a price. Were the players always happy about the wonderful pitch? Who asked them? Obviously they were thrilled even honoured to be playing at Wembley; the honour is unparalleled in English football. But did they like playing on it; did they get the best from themselves? How many Cup Finals were held up in the second half or extra time with players rolling on the ground in agony with cramp? You haven't seen that occur much lately and it may have given the commentators less to say but perhaps they haven't noticed yet. I bet the players have.

So, as you might guess, the pitch has a reputation, it certainly has an image to live up to, it is a brand of course with the Twin Towers, green striped turf featured on programmes and posters. The chain of bosses above me are justifiably sensitive to that and some are more conscious of a TV commentators unqualified criticism, than that of an international player whose opinion would have some credibility but rarely complain anyway. The player on the park is who the pitch is created for. I give them the best that I can, and they usually appreciate what goes into it at Wembley because they know what the ground staff at their own club do to get the best they can at home. Each ground, each playing surface comes with its own problems, the biggest being the frequency of games (which Wembley doesn't have) which prevents the staff from managing anything but crude repairs during a season. They are not all green stripes and flat, but it's not from the want of trying.

You could argue with much justification that plenty of players have criticised the Wembley pitch and I would agree, but usually the most publicised remarks have been wrung out of them and misquoted or taken out of context. Down on the pitch where I can listen, sometimes talk to the players before a game, I can't honestly remember such remarks, quite the opposite. But supposing they did complain, so what? They know their business and they have earned the right. I have on occasion been worried sick on reading that a player had 'slagged off' the pitch but then the player made a point of calling the office to let me know that they had said nothing of the kind. But by then it's been reported and some writers, who in general may be qualified amateur gardeners, have a job to find something to say and happen to have an enormous audience. Including the higher levels of officialdom at Wembley, most of whom know very little about how many blades of grass make up a football pitch but do know a lot about bad press. That's where the worry comes from, not the job, that's almost a pushover, it's from being constantly aware of what the experts might say and then waiting for the inevitable repercussions.

At this point, I ought to mention that in my opinion, which by now you might have guessed is I believe a reasonably qualified one. The Wembley pitch is not perfect, that's right, not perfect. It's pretty good, in fact it's usually very pretty good. But not always, it depends on so many things as has been mentioned previously. It's as good as it can be under the conditions and circumstances that prevail at the time and the outcome is down to me and I suppose, Almighty God who invariably wins these contests. It's also true that players, coaches, pundits do criticise, some more famously and loudly than others, they are not always misquoted.

I particularly enjoyed the international team manager being quoted as complaining about the grass being too long after a pundit had said he was concerned it was too short. It should be water off a duck's back, but it wasn't and isn't. The worry aggravated by frustration when not having the right to reply. ('don't go near the press Don'), is sometimes a bit much.

In my early years at Wembley, I hadn't realised the enormity of this kind of pressure, and I soaked it up, I was a sucker for any stick dished out from any quarter and took it personally and took it home. I believe and those who know me would say that I am a cool and calm person; it's not in my nature to lose my temper, just the bloke to have around in a crisis. Like many of my generation, I have dealt with enough horrifying events in the army, down the coalmines or in everyday life, which made any so called 'drama' at Wembley pale into insignificance, but it took a lot of years to get this into perspective. I am told that I didn't see it coming and unfortunately the mental strain, kind of crept up on me and a safety valve somewhere inside said 'pack it in' and finally blew its top.

1975 was an absolute cow of a year in many ways, what with the weather murdering the pitch and me trying to give it the kiss of life, most of the time I thought that I had bitten off more than I could chew and should have become a milkman. For what seemed an endless period, even when I knew that things were going badly wrong, I gave the impression that everything was under control, which it probably was but like a toboggan hurtling down an icy run. That is not what the hierarchy wanted to hear, but my demeanour hopefully stopped them from fretting and subsequently kept them at bay whilst I got on with the practical problems which were on the pitch.

I remember standing in the middle of the pitch one day with no-one to hear me but the silence that echoes around the stadium, looking at the ground, then up at the awful weather and saying a little prayer. I really did, I was brought up to believe though, that you can't pray for yourself, it's not allowed. Anyway, I did and perhaps Almighty God finally took pity on me or my long-departed father (a groundsman) had put in a few words but whatever the intervention, everything changed around. Within days the rain stopped, the frosts were gone, the work that had gone into the playing surface started to bear fruit. In a matter of days I could see a light at the end of the tunnel. By the weekend I felt great, a different atmosphere came over the stadium, the ground staff felt it too – there was a reason to turn up in the morning and we were so cocky with it. On the Sunday I decided to cut the pitch, something I rarely do, but the conditions were right and it needed doing, Jacky wasn't in and I wanted to see it at its best. I hadn't cut very much when I started to feel exhausted, which in itself was also strange as I had done very little physical work that morning and had had the best night's sleep for weeks. Then I got pins and needles in my arms and shoulders and I thought the big mower was getting the better of me, although it does most of the work it did vibrate like a demon. So I put it away at a suitable point in the cut and shortly afterward went home leaving the lads to lock up, I felt really rough.

Fairly obvious what is coming next, that night I was rushed to hospital, I'd had a heart attack probably on the pitch, and hadn't realised it. It was apparently touch and go for a few days although I don't remember much about it, they tell me that I technically died a couple of times but they had the equipment to cope. I do recall feeling very sorry for myself, thinking how unfair it was to get laid out just when things at the stadium were starting to go right. There had been times when I might have welcomed being struck down as sweet relief, but not then, not now we'd cracked it. If it was God's intervention he (or she) certainly moves in mysterious ways, I can't follow his (or her) kind of justice. I spent weeks in hospital but eventually, with a great list of instructions, was allowed home to convalesce. They gave me enough pills to open a chemist.

I had been having the odd telephone conversation with Jacky who kept me up to date on how the ground was faring under

91

the new conditions, but eventually I couldn't stand the suspense any longer. If anything was going to kill me it was the worry of whether or not I still had a job, I'd convinced myself that I would have to be replaced, the pitch and the fixtures weren't going to wait for me to get better. So, with something akin to going to my first interview, I asked someone to drive me to Wembley.

As I walked through the main entrance, I was spotted by the General Manager who came over to me and shook my hand warmly. He turned to a colleague and said, "We must be paying this man too well, I couldn't afford a suit that good". I was floored, I had barely stepped through the door and found that I was wanted after all and they were happy to wait until I was well enough to return in whatever capacity made sense. I had convinced myself that I'd been pensioned off or found a desk job, it was better than any of the tablets I'd been stuffing myself with for all this time. The mental relief was enormous.

Despite the fact that I wasn't really ready to return to work, when asked, I agreed to go to the Groundsman's exhibition at Worcester Park, Surrey. An event that I always attended. Listen, if the boss had asked me to put the goal posts up on my own, at that moment I would probably have tried it. Such was the feeling of elation that I hadn't been written off. So, I said certainly, I would go down there the next day and after seeing Jacky and the blokes who also made a fuss of me, I made my way home.

The next morning on the way to the exhibition I had got as far as Kings Cross tube station and realised that the incessant buzzing and deafness in one ear wouldn't go away. I'd promised to phone home to report my progress periodically (my Mrs was less than impressed that I was going at all) so I telephoned from the station and told my wife about my being deaf and the buzzing.

She wanted to know how I could hear her on the phone if I was so deaf and laughed her head off, typical 'Bet' (Betty), no sympathy.

I called her a soppy devil and said it wasn't funny, but I could see her point. I hadn't realised how deaf one ear was, but with my good ear against the 'phone the rest of the outside world in terms of sound had ceased to exist, it was horrible. She suggested it was wax or something and reminded me that the Ear, Nose and Throat Hospital was just along the road from where I was standing, 'they won't keep you long, there's no point suffering if they can fix you up in a few minutes'. I told her that I would give it a try and I'd let her know how I got on, I'd see someone if I could, then make my way to the Groundsman's Exhibition. Good job I'd made an early start.

I went to the Outpatients of The Ear Nose & Throat Hospital in Grays Inn Road and was told at first that I needed a letter from my doctor and an appointment. I was polite of course, told her I had neither, but could someone have a quick look anyway. They must have taken pity on me because after a while I was examined by a doctor. I remember muttering something about wax and answering all his questions, then he said "Wait there" and he went away leaving me to complete a few forms. Not long afterwards he came back with a nurse, took the forms and asked me for my home 'phone number. I said "Don't worry about phoning home, I feel well enough to get there all right". "No, Mr. Gallacher, you're staying here, so we need to call your wife to tell her, that's all". "Oh, bloody hell, not again", I only came in to get my ear un-bunged, I've got lots to do and the last thing I need right now is more hospital treatment.'

It was no good, as far as the doctor was concerned it was very serious and an operation to find what was wrong was vital, shen before I could protest further, I was stripped and put to bed.

"God, what is your ruddy game? What's my governor going to say about this? How long are you going to keep this up? He's not going to be sympathetic much longer, he'll think I'm a bloody invalid and put me out to grass, but not Wembley. Well, come on then, say something:" I never heard a thing, which may have been significant in itself of course.

In no time at all the doctors had my medical history and explained to me that although the exploratory operation they had in mind was a lengthy one, because of my recent heart problem they couldn't risk giving me a general anaesthetic. That's nice I thought what then? They said they would use a method whereby the system was 'frozen'; this meant that although I wouldn't feel any pain I would be awake during the operation. Charming: You know what it's like when a dentist messes around in your mouth and you imagine that he's using pneumatic drills and a pickaxe. Well, this was very similar except that he was drilling at one side of my head, as a consequence I didn't see anything to stop my imagination doing its worst.

Not only was I awake during the proceedings, I talked from time to time with the surgeon answering questions occasionally, but as time dragged on, the stress or shock that my body was taking began to tell on me and after being very ill on the table, I remember very little other than the desire to be gone from there, I'd had enough. I next remember being brought around in the ward with lots of people about me. At the time I thought 'That's a liberty; I wasn't allowed to sleep during the operation, now it's over you'd think they'd leave me alone'. What I didn't know until much later was that I'd been 'lost' again, and the heart specialists had been the ones around my bed.

"Listen God, I don't know if I'm supposed to be coming or going, will you kindly make up your mind". Nothing, not a word, I never heard a thing: I stayed at that hospital long enough to recover and have further tests; they fixed me up with a hearing aid for the duff ear and sent me on my way. I'd lost the hearing on one side, which I find very distressing from time to time, but having seen the pitiful cases, especially the deaf children in that hospital, it made me very grateful for what I'd still got, whatever its condition. So, I was able to return to Wembley, carefully avoiding the front door this time, and put in a few extra prayers to stay well for as long as possible. No chance.

The weeks of nothing to do but contemplate my past, present and future had left me with a totally different attitude towards the important things in life. I now realised that worrying about what people who didn't know any better had to say wasn't particularly relevant. I decided that by hook or by crook I did my job my way, because that's what I'd been employed to do, and if it was unpopular, so what? If I made a complete and utter muck-up of the pitch it would be put right - I could only get fired, but unlikely. There was no way that I would put my life on the line for the sake of Wembley Stadium, because I then realised that I'd be forgotten soon enough, whether I fought back, pushed off, or dropped dead, the games would still go on. So, I had the mental side straightened out, or as straightened out as anyone can with responsibilities, but the severe illnesses had left me vulnerable to anything going. The years of rotten working conditions (albeit self-inflicted) were now showing up, first with bronchitis, then pleurisy and then thrombosis in the legs.

That was made worse when chemicals going on the pitch brought me out in a rash, which in turn became ulcerated and so on and so on. For someone who'd been so bloody fit all of his life it was soul-destroying. I couldn't get a cold without something worse getting hold of me, I started to spend as many evenings at the doctor's as I did in my own house. It got to the point where the pills I was taking for my heart were being affected by pills taken for something else. In the end I stopped taking all the pills because they were confusing the symptoms so much, with their side-effects, that my doctors couldn't diagnose the ailment. Now I do without most medicines, I look out for my diet, hardly smoke, I barely drink at all. I'm aware if I'm overdoing it and I do all right. I have various complaints which get me down when they are acting up all at the same time, but it doesn't affect my work. I still get up at 6.00 a.m. every day to get to work by 7.00 a.m., I do nothing heavy, I don't need to nowadays, my work comes from my head and that's big enough to hold enough ideas to keep me at Wembley until I'm thrown out.

When I do retire, I don't want it to be because I'm too old or too ill, or because I'm a candidate for an early cremation, it's taken me fifty years to collect the knowledge I've acquired, I've got no intention of dropping dead before I've put it to good use.

"God, are you paying attention?" I said "I've got no intention of popping off yet, I've still got some things to do." Nothing - not a bloody word not even a tiny flash of lightning. So much for my religious upbringing.

I've wandered from the point again and now I've lost my thread. Oh yes, the moral of this story (if there is one at all) is that like many people, I put up with pain and discomfort that won't go away, it doesn't get better, it usually gets worse, and in my case it's because I didn't take notice of advice given to me by men who'd been groundsmen before I was born. So now I do know and as far as I'm in a position to decide, when it comes to my blokes working in heavy rain or taking shelter, they will have to take shelter. When it comes to spending hours on their knees in the wet, they will do so in moderation and only if there is no other way. If the powers that be don't like to see the ground staff standing in the tunnel apparently doing nothing, then they should stand out in the rain themselves and tell us about the results in twenty years' time, because that's when the payment comes due, but by then the deeds are forgotten. So, what's it all for? I'm not advocating a situation that we sometimes read about in certain industries, if you ask my staff they certainly won't think they're molly-coddled, anything but, they work damned hard, most of them. No, as long as time is on my side, I won't let the short-term benefits outweigh the long-term effects to man or pitch.

Bold words, Don, the only trouble is there comes a time when the rain won't stop, the frost won't melt and the job won't wait. Then and only then we'll just have to get cold, wet and tired, because the referee is going to blow his whistle to start the big match whether we are ready or not, so we are going to be ready. The weather has never beaten us yet and is not going to if I have anything to do with it.   There have been times when the weather has left us with conditions that we and the players didn't like very much, but it's never stopped a game and let down the paying public.

Hang on, I tell a lie, England against Bulgaria, November '79, but that wasn't the pitch, that was blooming fog - listen, that night we could have marked out a hockey pitch, the fog was so thick the footballers wouldn't have noticed the difference. It was dreadful, the fog had hung about all day and although out¬side in the streets it was reasonable (you could see across the car park) but in the stadium it was like a bowl of pea soup. Fifteen minutes before kick-off you couldn't see the goal posts from the half-way line and the referee called the game off.

It must have been a difficult decision, I talk about my pressure, that bloke took the responsibility to correctly cancel an international football match, with a stadium full of spectators and television and radio all poised to start.

'It's off', the referee announced.

As the television men scurried about looking for an old movie to fill the gap and as the disappointed spectators made their way home and even as the TV commentator made his apology to the viewers from the pitch, the fog disappeared. It just lifted up leaving a floodlit, perfectly marked out but empty pitch, what a cow, how can you credit it? I did think for a moment, that I heard the old sod chuckling from high above, but nobody will believe that, will they?

Note: The England v Bulgaria match was postponed for 24hrs

Don, Head Groundsman at St Ignatius Sports ground with Tottenham Hotspur East Stand as a backdrop. c.1955

In front of the pavilion during a cricket match between St Ignatius College students and college staff. Supplemented with Don Gallacher seated middle, plus brothers Frank, Robert & Terry standing immediately behind him

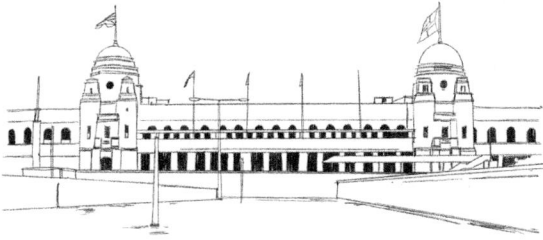

Chapter 9

Wembley Belonged to Scotland

The blood that flows through these old veins mostly come from my Scottish ancestors, for my father was born in Glasgow in 1881 as did our wider family and all we ever seemed to talk about when we were children in London, was Scotland. He would tell us stories of his childhood on Clydeside, of the gangs of kids always hungry, usually ragged, stories about the cobbled streets of Glasgow that fascinated and frightened. We got to know that world as well as our own, we learned of the poverty and the splendour and above all the pride that is Scottish.

Even at the turn of the century football was the national sport up there and my dad must have been pretty good when he was a boy. At a time when neither he nor his pals knew what it was to wear anything on their feet he was presented with a pair of football boots by a Scottish superstar of the day, his namesake Patrick Gallacher.

My old man played for a few Scottish teams, including Duntocher Hibs and Parkhead Juniors, but was eventually lured South to play for Tottenham Hotspur in London and whilst there he met and married my mother and raised six sons as big and braw as himself. When we were kids playing football in our street, which was just behind the Spurs ground in North London, it would be England v. Scotland. You know the way, coats as goalposts, a worn-out tennis ball, but as far as we were concerned Scotland were at home to England in Trulock Road. I'm not kidding when I say I've seen matches played at Wembley with less heat and determination than the way us kids played, it may have been a scruffy bunch with a make-believe pitch, but we played as though it was a full international match.

I well remember that when the Gallacher boys lined up for those street matches we were always the Scotland team, never England, Wales or Ireland, and to us in those days no other country played real football. In my time I always wanted to be a Scottish star, McGrory, Jimmy Simpson, Hughie Gallacher and many other great footballers. Never once did I want to be Arthur Rowe, Hapgood or any English hero of the day. It never occurred to me that I was anything other than a Scot, even though I was born in that very street in Tottenham with a London accent to match. It is only now looking back that I appreciate how strong my father's influence must have been on us and how deep the Scottish seeds had been sown.

All the relatives we knew well seemed to come from my father's side of the family, they were nearly all North of the border of course and although we didn't see them very often they were as familiar to us as if they all lived next door. Even in our front room, 'the parlour', you know the room that few 'ordinary' souls were allowed in, we had an enormous picture above the fireplace. Now in most Catholic homes, the best room would have a picture of the Madonna and Child there, or the Sacred Heart, or even Jesus Christ Himself, not our house. For although we regarded ourselves as good Catholics, we must have been better Scots, for in this special place was a framed photograph of a Scottish soldier, my father's youngest brother, Bobby and he looked rather splendid.

During the First World War in France, Uncle Bobby had posed in the uniform of his regiment, the Cameron Highlanders and it wasn't long afterwards at the age of 21 that he was killed. But Bobby would be remembered long after, for that photograph stood for all that was holy in our house and the pride that radiated from the face of that kilted warrior flowed through all of us throughout the years that followed.

We did go to Scotland from time to time and on one such occasion we went to see England play Scotland at the gigantic Hampden Park, with a crowd of 140,000. Us 'cockneys' shouted just as loud as any Scot there, we even wore tam-o-shanters, and the only 'troubles' on the terraces were between Rangers and Celtic fans arguing on who had made the Scotland team, but no violence was seen when I was there. Incidentally how many Scots have you met that didn't still have their accent, I never have. Even when they are far from home for donkey's years, it's always there. My father's brother, John, returned to England after 50 years in New Zealand. We met him at London Airport, expecting to be greeted with a strong New Zealand accent, but no. He was the last one off and the thick Glasgow accent called out 'Is there anyone here named Gallacher?' Seemingly half of the crowd put their hands up to greet Uncle John. From his accent you'd have thought he'd just arrived at Euston station from Queen Street Glasgow, not the other side of the world.

It was a Glasgow girl who became my first wife, she gave me my own family to raise, so then I had even more lovely Scottish kinfolk. What with all these relations but more especially with my father and then Peggy, my wife, that distinctive Glaswegian lilt was always to be heard in our house and even though they are both gone now I can still hear them when I want to.

Enough of this, I could go on and on if you let me, this preamble is supposed to be my way of showing you that I Donald Gallacher have a powerful affinity with Scotland, which I hold sacred and a love of the people which made the following that much harder to bear. This is the story of the day that Scotland came to town on the 4th of June 1977.

The Scotland against England game at Wembley is nearly always a game to be remembered, if not revered. The 'friendly' home international is a weird mixture of tension, excitement and rivalry on the park and on the terraces it's like no other game that's played there. The fans from Scotland always manage to look as though they outnumber the English supporters about three to one. Partly because of their fantastic display of colours, kilts flags and banners, partly because of their ceaseless singing, but mostly because they usually do outnumber the English three to one. These exuberant fans, many of them well-oiled by lunchtime, pour through the London stations and streets, and on up to Wembley, waving their banners, chanting their hymn 'Scotland, Scotland', convincing the Southerners that the Scots can and will beat anyone and everyone at football, 'and anything else, Jimmy'. A sad part of this enthusiasm is that some of the kilted warriors get so drunk when they get there they fall to the ground well before the kick off, just for a little sleep, never to see their heroes at all.

The last time the teams had met at Wembley, it had been a big upset for the Scottish fans, as despite the massive support, Scotland had conceded early goals and the England team had gained confidence, whilst Scotland had lost theirs. In the beginning the terraces were all golden banners and tartan tammies, and as usual all red-blooded Englishmen were trying hard to look like Scotsmen and were staying quiet. But after half-time, the terraces were hushed, barring the cat calls of the unforgiving Scottish fans, some of whom were going home, and the new-found voices of the Englishmen who, surprise, surprise, had been there all the time.

Two years had passed, but the humiliation was not forgotten, there was so much to play for and going by the roar of the Scots as their teams emerged from the players' tunnel, the fans could win this game all by themselves. England had a lot to play for too, they had lost at Wembley the other night, to the Welsh, the so called underdogs, now they were at home again, but it must have seemed they were at Hampden Park not Wembley. The Scottish fans never stopped singing their scornful songs, ceaselessly taunting every English touch, whistling at every action. Then when a free kick was headed into the England goal by McQueen, the big Scottish centre half, the stadium exploded, flags and banners, beer cans and caps went up in the air to rain down on the jubilant fans. The singing got louder and louder, it subsided only for a short while during half-time.alf.

Then Scotland scored again. This was too much for the fans to bear, they couldn't have wished for more. 'Two-nil, two-nil' they sang, over and over again, taunting and teasing right toward the end. A few minutes from time England were awarded a penalty, a deathly silence crept over Wembley, England scored and put the tails up the team, now supported by the few English voices. But they could hardly be heard as the end was so near and about 50,000 Scots were whistling so loud, encouraging the referee to close the proceedings and put everyone out of their misery.

Which at last, he did. - Scotland had won 2 goals to 1. The final whistle blew the signal that ended the match and started an invasion.

The pressure pot couldn't be contained any longer. The Wembley cauldron of bubbling porridge finally boiled over onto the pitch, tearing down fences in its way, within minutes the wild hordes of Scottish fans were over the dog track and onto the pitch, they poured over the ground in an uncontrollable mass, the teams and officials ran for their lives, most of them made it to the tunnel, the Scottish players that didn't were shouldered high.

In the time it took for me to get from the Royal Box to the penalty area, thousands were on the pitch, the goalposts were down, and the nets were shredded. All around me now were singing, screaming supporters, hurling themselves to the ground and upon each other in a frenzied dance of victory. Amongst the tartan mass, I could pick out other ground staff and stadium officials who had instinctively run to protect flag posts and goals, never realising what was behind them, they had never had to protect anything from anyone before and certainly nothing as frightening as this. I saw the familiar faces of my blokes swept along with the tide of tam-o-shanters, ashen faced and wide-eyed with shock, just as I was. This wasn't really happening, it had to be some kind of nightmare from which we would all wake up. But we didn't. Stretching up on tiptoe I tried to make out the far end of the pitch across the masses of heads where the other goals should have been, but I couldn't see them, they were down. I tried to push my way towards the players' tunnel, but the 'loyal' fans had the same idea and my way was blocked, I just stood there helpless.

I saw a policeman's white helmet with a familiar face under it, I yelled at the face under the helmet "For Christ's sake Geordie, where's the bloody horses ? Get the mounted police after these b......s ".

He said "I've just heard your people tell the commander to hold off, in case the horses' hooves cut the turf up too badly, but obviously, they'd shift this lot in two minutes:"

'Cut the 'turf up? What do they think 30,000 nutcases are doing out there? He said something else, but we were separated again and whatever it was, was lost in the noise. Cut the turf up? What nonsense, hoof marks can be lifted with a fork, these people aren't going to leave me anything to lift. At the top of the players' tunnel was a fragile barrier, now being defended against all odds by just three coppers, two WPC.s and four of our security blokes. The tunnel yawned enormously behind them, inviting the mob to march over the uniforms that meant so little to the higher authority of 'the mob'. What was so important anyway? Did these fools expect to take their team from the dressing room back to Scotland on their shoulders, or was it the Sassenachs in white they were after? Who could say, not me, not the poor sods defending that barrier, not even that mob, were the truth really known. In that atmosphere anything was possible.

I looked up the length of the pitch, the scarves and flags that had been on the terraces were now all over the pitch, they were there in their thousands, I couldn't believe my eyes. I saw a couple of blokes near me waving rags over their heads and just from the colour I knew they'd once been our corner flags.

There were grown men, fighting tooth and nail, over a segment of white goalpost, really thumping each other to snatch the spoils. A segment - how had the post become a segment? What was happening for God's sake?

One woman, she must have been fifty, wrapped in garish tartan, pushed two big lads over and snatched their souvenir from them for herself, it was a piece of goal net about as big as a scarf - that's how she wore it, on her head, and she danced with delight.

What the hell was going on? How could anyone tear a net with their bare hands anyway? How could metal goalposts be destroyed so easily, so quickly, ending up just a few feet long? The rabble had no tools, I was sure they had no knives, this wasn't planned, what kind of person was capable of such destruction with just bare hands? Or did they use their teeth, I didn't see.

The nightmare went on. I almost tripped over some old fool on his knees, I thought at first he was just another drunk pawing at the ground but no, he was tearing at the grass with his fingernails, he lifted a great big piece of turf out of the ground. I screamed at him "What the hell are you doing?" and pulled him to his feet. He staggered and looked at me flabbergasted, he wasn't a young yobbo, he was my age, anywhere else I would have said an ordinary bloke like me. He couldn't make out what the hell I was on about, he told me to push off and get my own bit of turf, there was plenty. He waved a hand toward the grass at my feet. "There ye are sonny, have a bit a Wembley to take home for the lads." It stopped me dead, he was right, what did I think I was doing, all around me holes were appearing in the pitch as divots were torn out by the roots, great clods of my turf were being thrown about. Who did I think I was, believing that I might stop this? I was fighting against thunder, thank heavens it was only a dream and we would all wake up in a minute.

After a while I could see that the way to the players' tunnel was thinning, I started walking towards it. Police were everywhere now, but the only ones having any effect were the ones on horseback, thank God they were finally here. I couldn't help thinking that history had repeated itself when the copper on the big white horse carved his way through the masses just as one had done here 50 years previously. The police were now coaxing the masses towards the terraces and exits.

Still the crazed fans held aloft their prizes of grass and posts and nets - it made me think of a picture I had seen in a book about the French Revolution and the prizes won by the mob around the tumbrels. The faces of the revolutionaries couldn't have looked more frightening than this lot. I pushed my way to the tunnel in a daze, I know I lashed out at those in my way, through sheer frustration, at the realisation that I was awake, that this wasn't a dream. My temper got the better of me when one 'butcher' tearing my pitch with his fingers presented his backside to me. I booted him hard, he picked himself up protesting, but probably too drunk to have been hurt. He told me I didn't have to kick him. I felt that I did.

I stood over him and said something inappropriate. In any other mob my pushing and shoving would have got me a good thumping, but not in this crowd, I reached the barrier unscathed. Somehow I knew that I would, for this riotous mob were in raptures over their victory, not vicious vandals, they were elated not enraged, they were absolutely, blissfully happy. I'd never seen such happiness.

In a while it was done, in less than an hour from the end of the match the madness fizzled out to a great big nothing, just another crowd pushing or being pushed toward the gates and the outside world. Some were dragged, half-carried by their mates, some, not many, were still waving their now bedraggled banners, singing at the tops of their voices, wanting the jubilation to last forever. But it was over, and all they got was their own noise echoing in that empty wreck that was now Wembley. I looked around at what was left, and came close to tears, that beautiful pitch, the centre piece of Wembley that had been made to look so good for the players and supporters, was now ravaged and abandoned like a spent battlefield and like most battlefields it had been used for a truly horrific purpose at a very high price for no particular reason.

What a field day the media had. They were on hand in great numbers of course, dozens of cameras, miles of film to record a very important football match. What they got instead, in glorious colour and using all the super lenses was a story that would make headlines on front pages all around the world. As the crowds dispersed, the photographers and reporters with nothing left but a massive story came looking for anyone in authority they could get a quote from, it doesn't usually matter to them who, anyone will do. Between sorting out myself, my staff and the occasional policeman, some idiot with a cameraman in tow shoved a microphone in my face and demanded of me my account of what had just happened. At that stage if my dearest friend had said 'Boo' to me I'd have whacked him or burst out crying. "How the bloody hell do I know what's happened? Weren't you here? Didn't you see it? Stop asking stupid questions and get off this bloody pitch. If you want information go and find the press officer, that's his job, push off and let me do mine." It was all heat of the moment, but at the time I meant every word, I just couldn't bear to hear any more of their inane remarks

remarks, no more stupid statements please, there'd been enough stupidity for one day.

From time to time I was asked by the police to identify 'trophies', each successive identification rubbed more salt into the wound. My ground staff who were every bit as bewildered as I was, looked for guidance. 'What's next boss?' There was nothing to tell them. At the end of the day there was little they could do and not much heart to do it with. Eventually as the pitch cleared, leaving just a few pressmen filming and our officials staring at it, I was wondering where to begin. I had to plan, but at that moment it seemed to be a futile ambition.

Whatever was to be done wasn't going to be done that night, so like dealing with the aftermath of an awful party, I decided to clear up in the morning. I couldn't bear to look at the pitch, the expressions on the faces of my blokes or talk to the press, and if I never saw a tartan tammy again, it would be much too soon. The Scots had come to town alright, and now they'd gone, gone with their noise, gone with their lunacy, gone with a big piece of me. My love affair with Scotland was finished, I needed a divorce.

That night at home I struggled to untangle my head, trying to figure out what had to be done to get things back to normal if, in fact, that were possible in the short term. I gave up watching the television it seemed to be showing the Wembley 'riots' at every opportunity. I wasn't to sit down for very long either being repeatedly called to the phone. I was grateful and took heart from the calls I had from friends and family who had seen it happen and had kindly thought of me. But they weren't the only calls I got that night. The 'media' 'phoned of course, just to get comments and confirmation, but worse were the 'nutters', the cranks who 'phoned me, then taunted and abused until I slammed the receiver down. The 'phone came off the hook. I went to bed and didn't sleep.

It was blessed relief when Sunday morning came, and I made my way to the stadium. At the time I travelled by bus and tube, and I took a lot of light-hearted 'stick' from my usual paper seller. His stall was a wonderful display of Sunday papers and almost every one featured Wembley on the front page, with enormous photographs. Whatever else was happening in the world most newspapers gave us the headlines:

JOCK THE RIPPER,
THE TARTAN TORNADO,
SHAME OF THE SCOTS,
THE TARTAN RIP-OFF,
WEMBLEY RAMPAGE.......

And photo on top of heart-breaking photo.

When I got to the station, my paper seller said "Wotcha Don, didn't they mess up your pitch then, never mind mate, you'll fix it soon enough". Said he thought the news was lovely, kept telling people that it was me in the paper. "Have your papers on me today, you're in most of them".

I thanked him, mentally noted that I'd be better off going home a different way for a few days and made my way to the stadium, a plan was forming. I'd seen so many photographs, so many newsreels that by the time I walked up the steps, I felt physically sick with apprehension of the reality that was waiting for me, I deliberately went in across the levels so that I would come out high on the terraces to overlook the pitch. I shouldn't have bothered. There isn't a camera made that could do justice to the scene before me. It was a mass of shallow craters from one end to the other, misshapen patches covered the 'sacred turf' and even the dog track was scarred and torn. Little stumps of mangled white metal jutted out of the ground where the goalposts should have been, the greyhound fence was still lying where it had been smashed down the previous day. Bottles and beer cans and garbage, a usual part of the aftermath, were this time all over the pitch, everywhere the eye could see was rubbish, it was a pitiful sight.

By the time I got my blokes organised I'd decided pretty well how I was going to achieve the impossible, that wasn't just to repair the pitch, any fool could do that. No, I had to repair it and to have it ready for a schoolboy international match in two weeks' time; this pitch was going to look the same way for those boys as it had yesterday morning before the Scottish fans ruined it. Looking around me it seemed long odds, but those young footballers deserved better from Wembley than this and I was going to bust a few guts to get it for them.

The blokes were sent off to their seemingly hopeless tasks, the priority oddly enough, was the rubbish on the greyhound track, it was a priority because there was a dog meeting scheduled for the next day and this wasn't ordinary rubbish. Just like clearing a minefield, my blokes went around that track on all fours picking out the slivers of glass and tin that was embedded in the turf, just waiting to slice the paws of those valuable greyhounds. Having got that under way I had a closer look at the craters didn't like it much and looked for something else to do. What's happening with the goal-posts? What indeed, short of explosive nothing seemed likely to shift these pathetic metal splinters that had once graced many a famous occasion. After half an hour the blokes had managed to get two of them free, but the other two wouldn't budge for love nor money, not cursing, not swearing and there was plenty of that to be heard. The original posts were oval shaped obviously slotted in an oval hole; now, thanks to the 'visitors', these two stumps were crossways, wide post in narrow hole and it wasn't going to move. It took hours of tugging and smashing and cutting and drilling to shift those swine. It didn't help the poor lads with hands cut and bruised when the 'experts' wandered on the scene and there were plenty, offering advice and pearls of wisdom. They didn't stay though - my blokes seem to have a way with words on these occasions, very discouraging they can be when the mood gets them, and the mood had got them like never before.

Now then, where was I going to get some replacement goalposts? I'd already 'phoned the importer at his home the previous evening to put him on the alert. The trouble was they came from Sweden and time was going to be the enemy, "Never mind," he said,' I promise we'll get them there on time, at least

113

Sweden isn't having a Bank Holiday tomorrow. Bloody Hell, the Queen's Jubilee, no-one was going to be available I would have to catch people at their homes. Reach out to suppliers, contractors and so on, now's the time to look for friends and sure enough they were ready to move. Although some of the repairs wouldn't be able to start until Wednesday, following the holiday at least the preparation would be well under way by then or so I hoped.

There was a hell of a lot to be done just clearing the place, the morning went in a flash and several times Jacky and I had tried to get to our cabin for a cup of tea, finally in desperation Jack made an executive decision "Sod 'em all" and we disappeared. Even up there we weren't free, a number of times my phone went, some calls were necessary, but some were bloody stupid. Continuous knocks at the door inter¬rupted our talks and meant cold tea again. Then there was yet another knock at the door which to Jack was the last straw.

"B..... off out of it" he shouted at the unseen pest. The knock was repeated, and I grudgingly opened the door. The pest, of course, (my luck) was the boss. "Don, will you come down to the pitch and talk to the Press?" What can you say? I left Jacky to his cold tea. Went down to the pitch again, this time with the General Manager, we walked toward a group of about thirty reporters and photographers. Some of them were quizzing and photographing one of the ground staff who was posing with a piece of turf in each hand. Good old Tommy I thought, trust him to play to an audience. Our Press Officer introduced the General Manager and the Head Groundsman to the Press assembled there. "Hang on" said one rather angry photographer, "Isn't this man the Groundsman?"

pointing to Tommy, still holding out his bits of grass and grinning like a Cheshire cat. They weren't pleased, but it soon got lost in the flood of questions and requests to pose in front of the scarred turf and so on. I listened and attempted to answer but was invariably interrupted with another question before I completed an answer, it was pandemonium and no wonder to me that anyone gets misquoted.

"Hold your horses" I said, " I want to ask a question now. "I've read this morning's papers, your papers, the descriptions of Wembley vary from 'sacred turf' to 'the finest playing surface in the world. My question is this – how did it become so lush and fine, when the same newspapers were slagging it off two or three weeks ago claiming it was a bloody disgrace? No? Well, I'll tell you something. You lot will still be reminding me of your hypocrisy when this Scottish nonsense is long forgotten". There was a long silence.

I thought the boss would have a fit. You're not supposed to say things like that to the press, they don't like it. Actually, it didn't much matter, they doubtless put it down to me letting off steam and asked some more daft questions.

"What'll it cost to put the pitch right?"

"I've no idea what it will cost I just have to put it right."

Actually, I had a fair idea, but I wasn't going to tell them. Not that that did me any good, I was still quoted as supposedly saying how much. The Press officer suggested a figure of about £5,000 for the pitch alone, but even that was quoted as high as £18,000. "What do you think of the Scottish supporters, is it true you referred to them as animals?"

"That's correct" I said.

"Don't you think that's a bit strong even in these circumstances?" pressed the reporter. "I don't think so" I said. "I was standing very close to many of them when I formed that opinion - if anything it's maligning animals, I think that I am regarded as an animal lover. Anyway, that's only a diluted version of what I really think and that's very weak compared to some of the headlines in your newspaper."

"How long will it take to grow again?"
What a dozy question. "The pitch will be repaired and playable in two weeks" I said, "in time for the schoolboy international England v. West Germany." Even the boss looked at me sideways.

"Are you serious?" said the questioner.
"Certainly" I said, "It's booked to be played here, nowhere else, the pitch will be ready for that game. It may not look as good as usual, (pause for effect) but it will play as good." Brave, brave words, Don, I thought to myself, even you're not absolutely certain, why give these blokes more ammunition?

Well, they were getting on my nerves a bit, I've got work to do. Anyway, I had made my mind up, it would be ready.

There were only a few more questions, a lot more photographs and they dispersed. Next there were interviews for the television news. I spent about 10 minutes with them answering questions then I got Jack, my deputy, to join in for the TV cameras. When they tried to film one of the ground staff repairing the greyhound track our Reggie wasn't too keen, I don't think it was nerves or anything, but he just wouldn't talk to them. The funniest incident I saw that day though involved some of the part-time gang known as the 'super-seven' and 'Tom and Jerry'. They may sound like cartoon characters, but they were a crucial back-up for stadium maintenance, especially after a big game.

Anyway, it occurred to me that the 'super-seven' were acting a bit strange. They were trimming out turf, but from their antics they were trying to work behind their backs. No matter what angle I saw them from I couldn't see a single face. Then it hit me, they were all trying to hide from the TV camera. Perhaps being casual labour, they were hiding from the taxman, or more likely they were avoiding being seen by employers or wives who didn't know they were there. Whatever it was, these blokes weren't going to be on 'News at Ten', even if it meant using a turfing iron behind their backs or upside down. I wished I'd had a video of those blokes that Sunday.

Now then, what about these craters? Imagine if you will, the pitch with holes on the surface ranging from several inches to as much as fourteen feet across and not all the same thickness, some were two or three inches, some were just skin deep. The shapes were hardly uniform either, looking down from the terraces the pitch looked like one of my kid's jigsaw puzzles, you know what I mean? A lovely picture spoiled by a load of missing pieces. My word, there were a lot of pieces missing. I knew that if I was to retain the quality and indeed the colour and avoid a patchwork quilt effect I needed identical turf. The same variety, same characteristics that had been just as lovingly cared for as the remains of the pitch I was looking at. As it happened I knew just the place to find it and it wasn't in Cumbria or any other far-flung part of the country that Wembley turf is reputed to originate. It was right under my nose; I was looking at it.

Behind each goal we have a grass area about 40 yards by 79 yards. These areas are cut and fertilised, at the same time as the main pitch, it was the ideal source of supply. We would take turf from there to the pitch and replace them with any turf bought in.

117

Meanwhile I'd received a telegram from my friendly turf supplier in Sussex, offering me whatever assistance I may need. It was a very welcome message I can tell you, so I knew I could get 'extra' turf quickly and time was never so important.

The way that I'd decided to fill in the 'craters' wasn't going to be easy, it wasn't like cutting out a nice, one foot by three-foot turf, as every hole was a different shape, every patch was going to be a different shape. I knew that wouldn't go down too well with the poor sods that had to do it either, it would probably take twice as long and twice as much skill. But if I had re-cut each hole to a uniform size I'd have needed 5,000 turf, not my estimated 2,000, and the result would have been the prettiest patchwork quilt ever seen on 'The Big Match'.

What a good idea Don: or put another way, go on then bighead, now let's see you do it: So, I did, and the job was started. Well, you can imagine, or perhaps you can't, take it from me, it was a fair cow of a job, but with a good crew, a lot of patience and a lot of effort we gradually grafted those pieces in place, over the next few days the jigsaw would be complete again. All that was needed then as an absolutely vital part of the 'cure', was for the patient to be lovingly nursed back to health and everybody kept off my pitch for about six weeks.
You must be joking Gallacher, if we kept everybody off for the next ten days we'd be lucky to have a playing surface for the Schoolboys International.

That's all right, someone said, there won't be a football match if we haven't got any goalposts. 'Don, phone your mate about the goalposts'. Don't worry said my friend, they had already left Sweden and due in Harwich in 48 hrs time. Well doe the Swedes.

118

Meantime, not to appear pessimistic but not wanting to be left looking like a lemon either, I phoned around a few mates. It turned out that the Swedish goalposts were different to everyoneelse's bloody goalposts. The only place that appeared to have our type of goalpost was in Scotland. If that wasn't poetic justice, I don't know what was. Anyway, thank heavens for good friends. My mate George Anstee at the Chelsea ground, Stamford Bridge said he could let me have a spare set of wooden goals that were almost (not quite the right size fitting that I needed and if necessary I could always have a carpenter re-shape them. Listen, if it came to it Jacky and I would stand behind the goals for the duration of the match, propping them up. Anyway, it was reassuring to know that we had a backup set if the new ones failed to arrive on time.

As it happened, a week later, the new ones were still having trouble clearing customs at Harwich and our poor importer who'd worked so fast, got them moving from Sweden on a weekend, arrived in England 48 hrs later as promised couldn't get the blessed things through the red tape at Customs. Whether it was the backlog of the Jubilee holiday or plain bureaucratic claptrap, the goals still weren't at Wembley the day before the match.

An air of panic crept-around the stadium from 'upstairs', as it wasn't known what condition the posts would arrive in; if they arrived, two painters were standing by and a driver had been told to be prepared to go down to Stamford Bridge for the back-up set: Never mind, the pitch was more than ready, I'd be happy for any team to play on it now, all the repairs had taken well, it was cut, marked and apart from a most unusual pattern I wasn't in the least bit disappointed, let's go to lunch. If the Swedish goalposts hadn't arrived by the time we get back we'll just have to go and get the wooden ones.

Incredibly, we never had to, when we got back the posts were there all 'gleaming white enamel'. That didn't stop them from being painted anyway I suppose as the painters had been waiting all that time, paint and brushes poised at the ready, the goalposts didn't stand a chance.

Saturday, 18th June 1977, England Schoolboys would play German Schoolboys at the Empire Stadium, Wembley, courtesy of Don Gallacher, Groundsman, with a lot of help from his friends. We walked out on the playing surface that morning with just a little bit of self-satisfaction about us. Not because it looked so good because it didn't, not for Wembley, no we were pleased that the impossible had been achieved, the boys would get their game and the 'knockers' would have to eat their words. The pitch looked great, or so I thought until a stadium engineer wandered over to us and pointed to the area behind the goal where the turves had been pinched for the pitch and replaced with turf from outside and told us that the grass was different shades of green there and could I do something about it.

I looked at him for a while thinking it was just possible that he wasn't really thick and stupid, and he was having a little joke with me. Well, he was, and he wasn't, but I was too disgusted to hit him or spit in his eye, so we just walked away. I believe he went on to oversee greater things.

The referee arrived and inspected the pitch thoroughly as always and thankfully he approved. So did the players, the managers, the Press, the TV. Commentators (and their guests, all the 'experts' studied the playing surface of Wembley that had featured on so many front pages and TV screens just two weeks previously. Now don't get me wrong, nobody said how wonderful it was. No-one actually suggested you could play bowls on it, but nobody actually criticised it either and that was good. The players, the people that it had all been for in my book, well they played their hearts out as usual, the school-boy international games are always good and this was no exception.

After the match I was pleased to accept the congratulations of various officials including members of the Football Association and also thanks from our Managing Director, James Harvie-Watt. It was nice to be appreciated from that quarter and I passed on his comments to everybody who'd worked so hard to make what was little better than a battlefield into the Wembley pitch that we were proud of.

I think it appropriate that this chapter should end with the deserved result: **Don's Team: Won – Scotland Fans: Didn't.**

SILVER JUBILEE YEAR INTERNATIONAL
for the
ESFA Sunkist Trophy

ENGLAND
v
WEST GERMANY

Saturday 18th June
Kick off 3·30 p.m.

WEMBLEY
STADIUM

Official
Programme
15 pence

TWO WEEKS LATER

Schoolboy International
England - 1
West Germany - 2

Headlines

WEMBLEY TARTAN RAMPAGE

by Mike Langley
Sunday People
Sunday, 5th June 1977

JOCK THE RIPPER

Daily Mirror
Monday, 6th June 1977

SHAME OF THE SCOTS

by Richard Stott
Daily Mirror
Monday, 6th June 1977

SUNDAY PEOPLE
Sunday June 5. 1997   Front Page
WEMBLEY TARTAN RAMPAGE
by Mike Langley

Wembley's hallowed turf lay in ruins last night. The worlds most famous soccer pitch was carved to shreds in an incredible riot after Scotland had beaten England 2-1. Frenzied Scots wielding daggers and dirks swarmed onto the turf in their thousands after the final whistle. And with the police looking helplessly on as the tartan army tore out the centre circle and both penalty spots.

Both goals – post, crossbars, nets and all – vanished into a heaving mass into a sea of tartan clad fans, almost certainly to reappear as souvenirs North of the border.

Daily Mirror Monday
June 6, 1977 JOCK THE RIPPER   Front Page

The massacre of England is over. And for one delirious Jock's joy, and Scotland's shame. For thrust above his head is a piece of Wembley....a great chunk of the hallowed turf mercilessly ripped to shreds by the tartan army after Saturdays international.
Until then it had been a day of good humour, with Scotland clearly outclassing England in a 2 – 1 win. Then came the final whistle, and mayhem. Thousands of plundering Scots swarmed on to the pitch. And in ten minutes of frenzied madness, they gouged out more than one hundred patches of turf.

123

Wrecked

Bottles and glasses were smashed all over the ground. Goal posts were broken beyond repair. Nets were wrecked and corner flags stolen. And the Scots were left to ponder how they won the match …. but lost respect.

Quote: Wembley Groundsman. Don Gallacher yesterday

'I've never seen anything so stupid. I almost wept when I saw what they were doing. They even ripped up the dog track.'

Daily Mirror

Monday June 6, 1977   spread over Pages 2 and 3

Shame of the Scots

By Richard Stott

Now the race is on to repair ravaged Wembley

The damage to the world's most famous pitch was put at £15,000 last night.

But soccer will pay a much heavier price for the ravaging of Wembley by jubilant Scotland fans on Saturday.

Groundsman Don Gallacher surveyed the wreckage and said 'It's a disaster. I've been a groundsman for forty years and have never seen anything like it'

Don said his team are now racing against time. They have to get the lush green turf back in perfect condition in less than two weeks for a schoolboy international game. But the devastation they face include:

More than 100 pieces of turf gouged out, wine bottles, beer bottles and glasses smashed all over the pitch.

Corks deliberately ground into the grass, razor sharp ring caps from beer cans pushed into the grass.

Goal posts smashed beyond repair, nets shredded and corner flags stolen.

Don said 'we'll have to work round the clock to sort this lot out. The glass is going to be the biggest problem. We will have to go over the whole playing area inch by inch. Just a sliver could seriously gash someone's leg.'

© Photo credit of Mirrorpix/Reach Licensing

Wembley groundsman Don Gallacher inspects the damage caused by the Scottish fans following the game against England

Jubilee People

OH WHAT A JAMBOREE!

JUNE 5, 1977   No. 4978   12p   ★ L

WEMBLEY TARTAN RAMPAGE

Victory Scots carve up pitch

By MIKE LANGLEY

WEMBLEY's hallowed turf lay in ruins last night. The world's most famous soccer pitch was carved to shreds in an incredible riot after Scotland had beaten England 2-1

Frenzied Scots wielding daggers and dirks swarmed on to the turf in their thousands after the final whistle.

And with the police looking helplessly on, the tartan army tore out the centre circle and both penalty spots.

Great hunks of turf—one measuring an amazing 8ft by 4ft — were hacked out and carried off in triumph.

Both goals — posts, crossbars, nets and all— vanished into a heaving sea of tartan-clad fans . . . almost certainly to reappear in little pieces as souvenirs North of the border.

Damage

Mounted police were called in, but they and another thousand officers on duty in the ground were swept aside by the tartan tide.

And within minutes the plundering Scots had caused an estimated £15,000 damage to the pitch.

One officer said: " It was absolutely incredible. It looks like the craters of the Moon."

Head groundsman Don Gallacher said: " I have never seen anything like it."

"They went mad,

Continued on Page 2

WRECKERS: Jubilant Scots fans rip down one of Wembley's goals in the pitch invasion.

A perfect start to the Jubilee holiday shindig when the Queen's horse, Dunfermline, won the Oaks yesterday. Now look at all the Jubilee goodies we've got for you.

THE QUEEN YOU DO NOT KNOW
PAGES 8 AND 9

THE OTHER JUBILEE
by the Queen of Jam City
CENTRE PAGES

Your chance to be QUEEN FOR A DAY
PAGE 15

JUBILEE FUN!
MAKE YOUR OWN ROYAL CORGI
PAGE 27

GLORIOUS BRITAIN
by Plain JOHN SMITH
PAGE 11

WHAT'S ON DOWN YOUR JUBILEE WAY
PAGE 13

PLUS 25 YEARS OF SPORT
PAGES 40 & 41

Patrick Gallacher player with Tottenham Hotspur 1904-05 (PJG top second left)

Patrick with 17th Middlesex Regiment. The Footballers Battalion WW1 (PJG top left)

Patrick on recently created sports field With Donald and brother Robert c1923

Don with brother Robert on St. Ignatius ground, Tottenham. c1923

Don on the ancient tractor with Spurs East stand in the background

Don with sons Colin & Donald on snow covered college field. c.1959

© Gallacher Family Archives

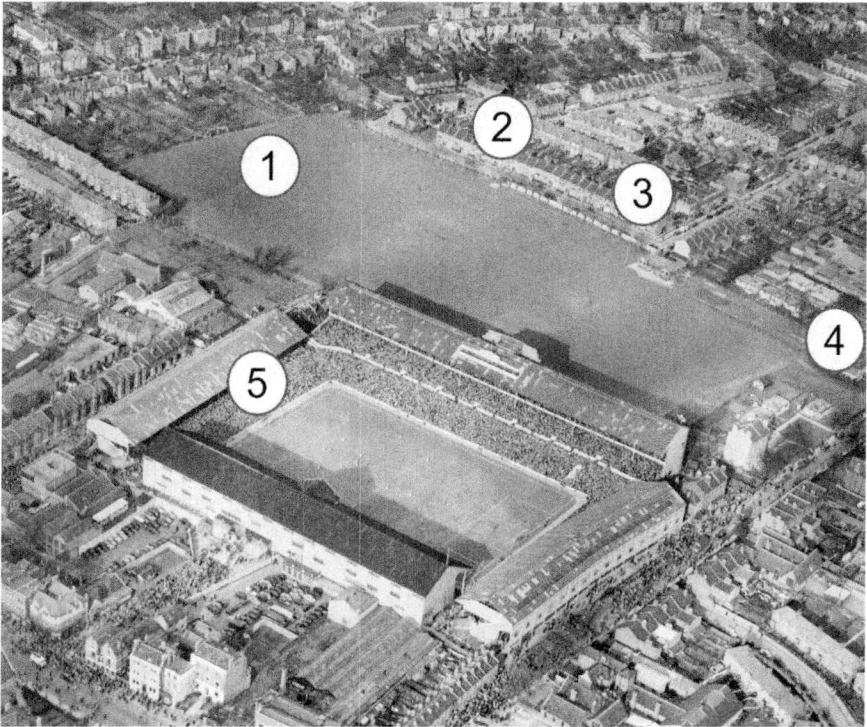

Aerial view of Tottenham Hotspur- Cup
semi-final. Chelsea v Arsenal, 1952

1) The field between Trulock Road and the Spurs ground had been part of a nursery, transformed into a sports ground by Don's father Patrick Gallacher, former Spurs player 1904-05, former, Footballers Battalion player/coach, 1915-18, creating playing areas on the Somme. Long term groundsman on the St Ignatius College field, the original West Ham stadium and elsewhere.

2) Patrick Gallacher married Alice Nicholson who lived in her fathers house at 7 Trulock Road, where Don and 3 more of his brothers were born and grew up. Alice met Patrick when serving teas to the Spurs players -1904-05.

3) Don's brother Robert later at 27 Trulock. played for West Ham, Leyton Orient and Hayes FC whilst employed as groundsman on St Ignatius field 40's-50's.

4) Don was employed as head groundsman for much of the 50's, 60's and early 70's whilst living at 125 Park Lane.

5) Tottenham Hotspur Stadium, not a million away from the one at Wembley.

Empire Stadium Wembley – Aerial View

© Alamy Stock Photo

A
Long way
to Wembley

© The Francis Frith Collection

Olympic Way

The Twin Towers Empire Stadium Wembley

"Only one pitch"
"But what a pitch!"

Live Aid Concert – Wembley Stadium 1985

A general view of Wembley stadium with the guard's band playing the National Anthem on the arrival of the Prince and Princess of Wales who opened the Live Aid concert. Saturday 13 July1985

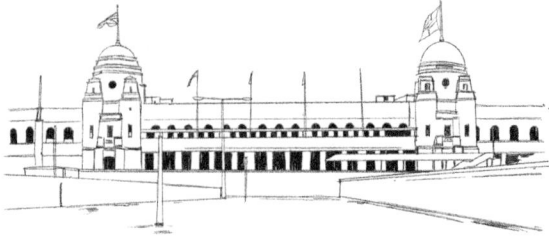

Chapter 10

The Grand Tour

As you probably know, millions of people watch events at Wembley from all around the world by way of television. Hundreds of thousands more pass through the turnstiles to watch their teams play football or rugby and thousands travel there to see a pop group or rock band. But you may not know that almost as many thousands come to see Wembley when there is nothing on the pitch but grass and maybe someone cutting, repairing or marking it. If you are not among the aforementioned number, I will be glad to offer a brief insight into why they do that. Welcome to the Wembley tour 1977.

When you arrived at Wembley Stadium to join the tour you are directed to that massive frontage with the world-famous Twin Towers and specifically to the huge double doors that open onto the Royal Tunnel. Each side of these doors are plaques on which you can read the winners of all the events at the Olympic Games held there in 1948; many people stand and study these names possibly recalling stars of yester year. Also, in that area you would see the plaque stating that the 1966 World Cup was played at Wembley and England beat West Germany in the Final. Who doesn't know that?

Let me guide you up the wide steps, which are each side of this frontage, that lead up to a platform in front of the Banqueting Hall between which are flower beds and in the middle of that is the original rostrum that held the Olympic flame in 1948. Impressed? Interesting enough but we must move on. The entrance for all tours is on our right and a pleasant member of the tour staff will greet you, take the entrance fee and introduce you to your guide. But on this occasion it's just me and you will just have to use your imagination. The tour starts with a look at the Trophy Case; most of the beautiful cups and shields in it belong to the 'Lions' Speedway Team world famous for so many years, the more notable cups aren't here, they are usually kept by the clubs that won them.

Leaving the Banqueting Hall and go through a door onto a part of the Stadium known as 'The Levels' in fact this is 'B' level. I can best describe it as a wide indoor roadway that runs around the Stadium underneath the top section of 'The Stands' (which are actually seats) and it is big enough to take the largest of lorries. Each side of this roadway are the entrance gates and doorways to all of the various sections of the seating and standing accommodation. On the Levels we also see a multitude of small units: Programme kiosks, hot dog stands and numerous bars and refreshment blocks, all closed today of course. The guide will take you along the level to the first aid centre, not for treatment, you've not walked far enough yet to need that, but part of the building houses a cinema. About 15 minutes is spent looking at films of the great games of the past and many different shows that have been put on at Wembley: Boxing matches for world titles, a Russian circus, pop concerts, and religious gatherings. Wembley has exhibited so many different things it is hard to remember them all and the film show gives an insight into the amazing range of events that are held there.

As a matter of interest this room is also used for some TV interviews, usually the one where players and managers are interviewed after matches, so the back wall may be familiar to many of you.

Out of there and down the steps, still inside the building, we haven't seen the outside world since arrival. Past the official dressing rooms where many famous referees have changed before taking charge of the match. Now we are on the ground floor and moving into the bathroom comprising slipper baths, showers and toilets and a huge plunge bath which takes about four hours to fill to a depth of about five feet. Short players are provided with water wings. This is the one place that looks enormous even by Wembley standards, but fill it with dirty, sweaty exhausted players and support staff, add some shouting, singing, sometimes a little crying and it's not that big at all.

From the bathing floor and up a short ramp takes us to the door of the dressing room. We are now in the North Dressing Room, these dressing rooms have changed over the recent years. Before the improvements the dressing rooms were much too big and draughty and the ceiling was high enough to fly a kite, it must have been like getting changed in a concert hall. We're much more homely now with suspended ceilings and the floor has a covering that is no longer cold mosaic tiles, it's a fitted carpet much better for bare feet on a winter's day.

All around the room there are jerseys of most of the Football League clubs. Complete strips of some and photos of the famous and not so famous. There's also a pair of football boots that must have come from the days when skulls were kicked around, I think

I have a pair at home myself somewhere. It's hard to take it all in and all the time you are gazing in wonder the guide provides information, facts and anecdotes, telling you so much you may find it difficult to remember everything. But don't worry, the brochure will feel in gaps later on and you wouldn't be the first to come back another time.

Let's move out into the big and often windy players' tunnel, directly opposite is the South dressing room it's the one that the England team use now. You may not be aware of this, and the guide isn't meant to say, but the North Dressing room is regarded as the 'unlucky' one, I suppose the statistics have borne that out but I haven't looked. On that note, for FA Cup Finals the decision as to who gets the 'lucky' dressing room is made alphabetically, so you work it out.

By now you can finally see daylight, in fact the light is literally at the end of the tunnel. Your guide will ask you to wait at the bottom of the long ramp while he walks to the top of the tunnel. He throws a switch and inserts a key, and then moves on to the barrier at the edge of the greyhound track. He beckons you to walk out into the sunshine (if it is) and as your group reaches the top your ears are blasted with a recording of a mass of people singing 'Abide with Me' it's very effective and to many, quite emotional and will give you an idea of the experience felt by teams on match day.

Actually, it's barely a fraction of the noise that the players hear when they come out of that big opening but it's still a wonderful exhilarating moment during the tour. Mind you the ground staffs hears it so many times it passes unnoticed, in fact 'Abide with Me' no longer brings tears to my eyes, it's more likely to get on my nerves. Then, unlike reality, the sound is switched off and the silence is so sudden it's absolutely deafening. Oh, that we could turn off the noise from a real crowd so easily especially when tribal singing competes with say, a national anthem.

And there it is in front of you, Wembley Stadium from the inside, the stands, the famous roof with its Twin Towers and the even more famous Wembley pitch all green and shaded stripes just like the picture on your brochure except now you can smell it as well. But by now you are probably too busy posing for or taking photos to notice it in isolation of everything else.

What is often forgotten about Wembley is that around the pitch is a greyhound track and one of the first things that your guide will show you is the hare rail that runs around it. Immediately above the players tunnel there is a box, and the guide lifts its lid to reveal a black and white hare, stuffed of course but it looks real enough for a bunch of dogs to chase after on race nights. I think this one is called 'Horace'. Your guide will tell you about the greyhounds and the track, changed over from turf to a complete sand circuit in recent years. Before that I used an average of 22,000 turves every year to keep the grass track in good repair, which is an awful lot of grass, now all we need is an awful lot of sand.

The TV gantry high up in the south side roof will be pointed out to you. The BBC used one end, ITV the other, with camera positions and commentary cubicles in between, it's a pretty big box suspended up there and probably the best view in the place but not a seat for anyone concerned about heights. They tell me that on a big match day the TV companies use nearly 100 miles of cable one way or another and I can believe that as I have tripped over them on many an occasion.

Under the roof on the North side, we have what is known as the press gantry, the centre section is for stewards for greyhound meetings and the man who drives the hare is also up there. He's the one that makes the mechanical hare stay in front of the dogs, it must drive them stark staring mad, but they keep trying. On big match days the stewards' box is used for radio commentary and obviously representatives of the press use this gantry too. The large electronic board at the far end of the stadium is the tote, and above your head over the Players Tunnel, another electronic score board which nowadays spells out messages of all sorts to the crowd and is operated from the press gallery. I suppose in time we'll have American style score boards with 'Space Invaders' images shouting 'GOAL' especially for those spectators that aren't able to work it out for themselves.

Walk across the dog track onto the red shale, which is the only sign of the speedway track that exists when it is not wanted. Beyond that is a rope to stop you walking onto the pitch, it's no longer allowed. It was when the first tours began but the pitch was being worn out and I'm sure visitors wouldn't like to see the famous pitch with pathways across the ends. Even the stone of the mighty Acropolis was worn out by visitors, my pitch stood no chance. Sometimes I am called over to talk to the people, and if I have time, will answer questions but as much as I quite like doing that it's not always possible, I'll tell you more about that later.

When you have listened to all the very interesting things told to you by the guides, you return to the path that runs around the greyhound track and make your way to the Royal Tunnel. The short walk puts you closer to the famous Wembley turf than any spectator at any game can ever be and most people just stop and stare. I would like to think they are wishing they all had a lawn like that. Then after a brief talk you will be invited to walk up the steps to the Royal Box, just as the players do at the Cup Finals and although you won't be jostled and congratulated by eager fans as you climb the steps, we do have taped sound effects to give atmosphere. At the spot where the guest of Honour normally sits you are given a cup to hold aloft as you have seen so many football and rugby captains do. Oh, I mustn't forget the Women's Hockey and other events, they have much coveted honours too, delivered in much the same way.

But on this occasion it's probably one of our speedway final cups. Have your photograph taken by a friend with you holding a cup at Wembley, back down the other side to the pitch level, sit on the red seats where so many famous players and managers have sat and when you are all assembled move into the Royal Tunnel. All that should be enough to impress most people but there's more to come. Inside again and through a door which takes you up to the Royal retiring room with décor designed for Royalty, then further out into the Royal box to sit where the VIP's sit and look down as they do on match days. It's the best seat in the house Mrs. and worth every penny, even if on the day it's only to watch my staff working on the pitch. Your guide will answer your questions and talk yet again and only when you are satisfied will he move you up to the Tour Shop for tea or coffee and the chance to purchase from many wonderful souvenirs something that will remind you of a memorable day out.

Right, that's the promotion over, now let me tell you about my side of the tours, how I affect the visitors and how they affect me.

As the last strains of 'Abide with Me' echo around the stadium, I'm aware that a tour is on its way and if I'm in range and have a few minutes to spare, I will walk toward the track near to the tunnel. The lads who take the visitors around know that sometimes I really can't stop and talk but I will if I can and they always look towards me for a nod or a wink, they usually get the message. Actually, I'm not officially supposed to stop and talk to anyone, but the tour lads appreciate my comments to the visitors and I'm always glad to chat about the pitch.

Sometimes I'm introduced with such an embarrassing build up that I have to spend a few minutes proving I'm normal or nearly normal. "This is our very famous Head Groundsman, Don Gallacher, who is regarded by some as the ...." and so on. Fortunately, I have a warped sense of humour and head full of clichés and useless anecdotes to get me out of trouble. Well, they do usually.

The visitors are invited to ask me a question which often bears no relationship to my job at all, but I don't mind. Most of the queries concern the pitch, usually it's to tell them the secret of keeping up a high standard, it's not easy to accept they can't have a lawn like Wembley, but I often suggest that it's not necessarily a good idea to have a football pitch for a garden and that's what they would have. It's a pleasure to answer the occasional technical enquiry and I do get them from time to time. The trouble is, this takes up their precious time and most of the other tours would get bored hearing about the varieties of grass and fertilisers, so I try to vary the conversation and keep it light. Actually, the questions are very sensible as a rule, especially those from the children, they are the ones that catch me out if anyone does. I remember one lad who was with a school party, he told me that he had seen my on the television once.

"Oh yes" said I "was it the Cup Final?" "No" he said. "It was Multi-coloured Swap Shop; You were talking to Keith Chegwin on the Pitch". That's right I remember doing that programme, but

I never saw it because it was live one Saturday morning. "I saw it' he said,' But you're different in real life, you're a lot fatter than when you are on the tele". Out of the mouths of babes!

We get a lot of school parties, groups of Scouts and Guides and it's always a pleasure to see children getting an education in this way. Another group I like to see are the 'Little League' Football teams on tours. If you run a team and write into the Tour Office, your team can come along wearing their own football kit and be photographed collecting the cup from the Royal Box. Not a bad picture for the scrapbook and it gives the youngsters a taste of what could be, there's nothing like starting them young.

The infinite variety of nationalities on a typical tour always amazes me. The foreign visitors make up a large proportion of our tours, and we get the most curious questions from them. The Germans invariably ask the same one each time. During the World Cup Final in 1966, Germany claimed to have scored a crucial goal, which hit the crossbar down to the ground and out again. It was disallowed. Fifteen years later I'm still being asked to point out which end it was, even when the goal posts aren't up. As it happens, in true Gallacher fashion, with only two ends of the ground to guess from (I wasn't quite sure at the time) I chose the wrong end, still, it's only a technicality, but it's the sort of thing that they seem to take seriously because they believe it cost Germany the World Cup. I suppose the English fans still talk about 1966 it as though it were yesterday.

It is incredible how famous this pitch is, but of course the big games are televised in countries right around the world and are seen as often abroad as they are seen here. Subsequently, the Wembley pitch is as familiar to an Australian or American as perhaps someone from London or Liverpool, and this is demonstrated by the warmth and enthusiasm shown from visitors abroad.

Unexpectedly, i've made a lot of pen pals through the tours. I hear from people all over the world who've met me at Wembley stadium while on a guided tour around the pitch. An Australian couple, Gerald Burge and his wife were on holiday in England and as a football fan he had to make for Wembley, he left the group and came across the shale and asked me to autograph his Wembley book. We chatted for a while about the grass and the games held here. He told me a little about Australia and then I sent him on his way before he missed the grand tour, he hurried after the group, who were by this time making their way up the steps to the Royal Box and that was the last I saw of him. I'd enjoyed the chat and was pleased to meet such a charming couple but thought little more about them until the following Christmas, when we received the most delightful card from sunny Australia. It was of course from Gerald Burge and his wife, who had taken the time to remember us; it gives you a nice feeling all over when that sort of thing happens, and we still correspond.

I also receieved a lot of mail from students with quite elaborate enquires related to subjects they are studying. These, as with all the letters I receive, get a prompt factual answer, but if they wish to see or visit me at the stadium I usually direct them to John Feenstra (tour manager) and he ensures that they have parent's permission (if it applies) and they get to know the best way for them to join a tour.

There was a group of visitors recently who had come up from Wales for the day and they wanted to ask a few questions. During the proceedings I asked where they had come from "and don't say 'Wales', that's obvious." We're all from the Rhondda was the reply "Come on" 'I said, "whereabouts in the Rhondda?" They rattled off

142

several Welsh villages and towns, including one call Ton Pentre'.

"That interesting" I said, "My father played football for Ton Pentre". "Go on boy, when was that then"? "I don't know" I said' "it must have been about 1914, I suppose." You should have seen their faces. "Bloody hell, you're kidding, nobody played football in those days did they?" "Cheeky devil!" I said I wasn't kidding at all; it must have been about then because it was towards the end of his playing career. The trouble was that I doubt if the oldest one there was more than thirty-five. So it might as well been 1066 as 1914. Nonetheless some of them went back home determined to find someone who was old enough to remember my dad. Ah well it makes life interesting doesn't it? Look, if you're not going to pay attention I won't' bother to go on and believe me I do know 'how to go on'.

What about the Japanese gentleman then? John Feenstra pointed him out to me because he had lots to say but none of us could understand a word he was saying, his excitement was so intense we thought he was on medication. He dashed about all over the place looking at everything and waving and pointing at anything that caught his eye, just like a kid in a toy shop, he couldn't contain himself for the thrill at being at Wembley. We had to physically restrain him from going on to the pitch, he so wanted to get out there.

From his reactions you would have thought he was a football fan whose team had just won a Cup Final, but there was nothing on the pitch that day to get worked up about, only Jacky..... enough said!

He jabbered away in Japanese, I nodded or shook my head not knowing which to do for the best. He ran up the steps to the Royal

Box and took dozens of photographs then he persuaded someone to take dozens more photographs of him using his camera. Then he ran down, set his camera on a tripod, presumably on a timer and ran up the steps again to take a picture of himself holding our speedway cup over his head. He was like a man possessed the way he galloped around. When he got to the tour shop, according to the blokes he spent a small fortune on Wembley souvenirs, and you have got to go some to spend a fortune in there.

Then the poor man passed out. Well apparently everyone was panic-stricken, took him to first aid and did was expected, but fortunately he'd only fainted and soon came around with a big smile on his chops. He was thought to be seriously ill, but an organiser with his party explained that the man had wanted to see Wembley Stadium more than any other place on the itinerary and the excitement had just been too much for him. Did you get that? The excitement at going to Wembley Stadium had been just too much for him!

I wished I could get that worked up when I arrive in the mornings. I'd be finished by 10.00 o'clock. It just goes to show though how a place that in the main, the most of us take for granted or criticise, is held in such awe by some of the visitors. I suppose that applies to all famous places, I bet the Eiffel Tower is a place where very few Parisians go for a holiday, and it probably blocks some Parisian's light out or something. You can't win can you?

Sometimes I see people that I have known from years ago, but don't immediately recognise them. They, however, are told my name and even though I'm looking ancient the name and a slight resemblance to the gorgeous thing that I used to be jogs their memory. It's sometimes a mutual shock I can tell you when it's been twenty or thirty years since I've met some of these old friends. This renewing of acquaintances has happened quite a few times and in the main I'm very pleased when it does, there are the odd embarrassing exceptions, but I won't enlarge on those.

During a tour a while ago a man introduced himself to me, he was a pal of mine from our boy scout days, can you image me as a boy scout? Well, I was. This chap even introduced me to his grandsons who were with him on the tour. I had to tell him that I'd acquired quite a few grandchildren of my own since we'd last met. Come to think of it half of them are probably working by now; if they're not I hope they will be soon, it may come in handy.

Another time a gentleman patiently waited for an opportunity to speak during question time, but instead of a question about Wembley he said "Are any relation to Jack Gallacher, he's got two sons Donald and Brian." I said "yes, he's got a daughter named Daphne too, I'm Donald, Jacks my eldest brother." That's all he wanted to know really, he said he'd asked because I looked like him, he knew all my family, unfortunately I didn't know him from Adam and he didn't linger, just shook my hand, wished me all the best and re-joined the group

This sort of meeting with the public because I am working, is usually confined to short exchanges between us. But one quite recently, I would have liked to have prolonged. It happened during a visit which was made up from a party of senior citizens out on a day trip. As 'Abide with me' heralded yet another tour group coming out of the tunnel, I let it be known I was there if I was wanted and sure enough I was called over to be introduced and asked to answer the visitors' questions. As sometime happens it was more general conversation that got around to the FA. Cup Finals and the teams that have played at Wembley. Somebody said how marvellous it would be if one of the underdogs succeeded in getting to a final and maybe even winning the cup. I agreed we had seen some good games here in the amateur cup matches and from what I'd seen on television, teams like Enfield or Aldershot played just as entertaining a game of football as any so-called super-team.

One old gentleman piped up "Good old Aldershot! That's my local team I don't suppose you've ever been to their ground; it doesn't look like this". I said I hadn't been there lately, but I knew the town of Aldershot from my time in the army, in fact I'd spent some time on my back in the Cambridge Hospital there, "mind you!, I said it was some time ago, 1940 actually". "That's a coincidence" he said, "I was in the Cambridge Hospital in 1940 I don't remember you though" and laughed. "I'm not surprised", I said 'there were quite a few of us there weren't there, I was in the Coldstream Guards at the time."

The tour moved along, probably bored with two old twits going down memory lane. We continued our conversation as we walked, and the elderly gentleman and I swapped tales of the hospital in Aldershot during the war as we followed the tour around the track, and we tried to bring to mind any mutual people from that time. He then said that he could recall two guardsmen when he was there; he thought they might have been Coldstreamers. One in particular he said, was a real sod, always getting the nurses at it, playing tricks and generally making the patients laugh despite their misery. He clearly recalled how this guardsman had made a monkey out of him by talking him out of his chicken dinner. At a time when the patients who could eat were served up typical army fare, this man had a special diet for his complaint and on occasions it was chicken. Virtually unheard of in the average diet during the forties, he said and of course I knew.

He continued with his memories and recalled that the comical guardsman somehow convinced him that he'd seen the awful conditions in the kitchens and the chicken especially was a bit suspect and certainly too risky for his weak condition. The man was so taken in by the story that he couldn't face the chicken at all and eventually let the guardsman disposed of it for him without the nurse finding out. Needless to say, that whilst he made do with a scrounged boiled egg for his dinner the guardsman and his mate scoffed the supposedly dangerous chicken. I got the impression that this was a tale that had been told in his family circles a few times, but not lately, this was ancient history.

The visitors were disappearing around the track with the tour guide but by then completely forgotten by myself as I felt the hairs on the back of my neck lift and some long-forgotten memory brought goose bumps on my skin. He went on about the hospital and the guardsman whom he remembered quite vividly now, until he finally told the story of how the young soldier had half a missing index finger and he was always making the patients shriek with laughter when he used to pretend that it was a normal length finger jammed up his nose or stuck in his ear. He smiled at the memory and looked at me to see if I remembered him too or just found it funny. I couldn't talk, I just nodded, as a lump swelled my throat and with tears in my eyes, all I could do was hold up my left hand, the one with only half an index finger, the one I still trick my grandchildren with by getting it stuck up my nose or in my ear.

I turned away not wanting him to see the tears running down my cheeks, God alone knows why it affected me so much. This man had unlocked a picture of the young men that we had been forty years ago, so strange to us that we didn't associate them with who we were on this

147

day at Wembley Stadium. What a very small world this is.

There was no more to say, and I couldn't have said much anyway, we shook hands, and he went off to join his party, presumably with a new twist to his old tale. I didn't know the man's name in Aldershot in the 40's and still don't know it now. If he is still with us and he or his family reads this, do please get in touch, I will try not to cry.

To mark the occasion for when the tours had the 50,000th visitor it was decided to do something a bit special. The captain of Ipswich and at the time England too, was a smashing bloke named Mick Mills and he had agreed to meet the lucky person. Bear in mind now that the tours had turned out to be family affairs, it wasn't just the little boys and big boys that come to Wembley, in fact they tell me at the moment it is 70% Male and 30% Female, so it could be anyone. As it turned out the counting stopped in the middle of a Cub Scout group and the cub that was greeted by the England skipper and the photographers was a little lad called Simon Edwards. Mick presented him with a football for a keepsake and then gave him the real FA. Cup to hold and have his photo taken with. The trophy had been won by Ipswich that season and Mick had kindly brought it with him. Then after more photographs, this time in the Royal Box, they came out onto the pitch, cub pack and all. I was introduced to Simon and even more handshaking. Simon was asked if he had any questions for the Head Groundsman and I thought I knew all the answers but I didn't know this one, he absolutely floored me with ; "how does the tote box work?"

Now it's not that often I get struck for an answer, but this was something I knew nothing about, and I felt a right twit, so my part in the proceeding fell quite flat. Still, it wasn't too important and somebody came up with the answer anyway and he more than had enough to make his day one he'd remember. I daresay he has a photo just like the one I have in my house, it's a picture of Mick Mills, myself and a smashing bunch of cubs in the middle of the pitch, it's a picture I will cherish.

For the 150,000 visitor, Wembley wanted to go one better and they arranged to have Kevin Keegan and Sir Stanley Matthews in attendance. International superstar Kevin Keegan was in England and was available but Sir Stanley was on a tour of the USA on promotion of Youth Football, typical of the man who devotes so much of his life to the teaching of new players. Nevertheless, he said would come. He arrived in this country around noon and by two in the afternoon was at Wembley eager to get out there with those lads. Again the lucky person was a young man (and it wasn't contrived either). On the pitch we had many sports writers, press photographers and various officials. One of the photographers started to lark about with a football while they were standing around waiting. I told him to pack it in, it wasn't the local park, but the boss told me to overlook it for once. What he didn't know was that I wouldn't have minded a kick around myself, but rules are rules, and I won't let me do it even though I may have aspirations to play at Wembley too. Or anywhere!

Then they were there, the men of the hour. Coming up the tunnel the captain of England Kevin Keegan and the legendary Stanley Matthews, they were leading two teams of visitors including the star of the day Paul Smethan the 150,000 visitor on a Wembley tour.

Many V.I.P's waited to greet the teams and the photographers took their pictures. Sir Stanley spotted me in the group and came over and shook my hand. Then they moved out onto the turf. The real guest of honour, young Paul Smethan, was a bit over-whelmed

149

I think, not surprising, it was a real good day made more so by the superstars. We were all privileged to see the greatest winger of all times make a run down the wing at Wembley, to put a perfect pass to Kevin's feet. That man could play in any team in the country even at his age; seeing those skills bought back memories from over 30 years ago when I had played against him. How come he's so lovely and fit and I'm so horrible. We talked awhile about the pitch and old times and posed for a photo or two, magical moments for my scrapbook, then everyone went to the tour shop for lunch.

My last glimpse of Sir Stanley was of a very tired gentleman, still answering questions and signing autographs with a smile and a word for everyone. Despite his obvious fitness he must have been feeling the effects of a very long day, but he stuck it out for the kids just as long as they wanted him to. I had nothing but admiration for that man and his partner for the day Kevin Keegan, who will doubtless go down in the annals of the great footballers of all times and I am sure he will be held in the same regard as Sir Stanley Matthews for his genuine concern for others. What a smashing day for all us kids!

So perhaps you can see how the tours concern me. On the surface it may seem like a group of people passing though the stadium, a tiny part of my job, barely anything to do with me at all really. But I have some laughs, meet some lovely people, made everlasting friends and discovered long lost pals. It will be an aspect of my time at Wembley which will have a more lasting effect on me than any of the big names or big events rolled together.

It's also nice to know when the critics are having their say that people come from far and near to see Wembley Stadium, not even for a match or a rock concert, they often come back more than once, and they are usually thrilled at what they see. It does show that it's not everyone who thinks that Wembley's a dirty old dump. To our visitors it's something special, it's regarded by players from all over the world to be the 'Home of Football' and although the stadium is a bit frayed around the edges it's still the best pitch in the world.

The stadium is maybe looking her age now but so are all of us who have been around as long: My word, if walls could talk this old girl could tell some stories, who knows, perhaps if I'm there long enough I'll get to hear some of them.

Don with the legendary
Sir Stanley Matthews, CBE

Correspondence from former Tour Managers

On Friday, 3 April 2020, John Feenstra emailed Don's son and co-author Colin Gallacher.

Hi Colin,

Lovely of you to send this over, it brings back memories!

I remember your father very well, a great man. He and his assistant 'Jack', can't remember his last name, were instrumental in helping us set up the tours in those embryonic days in 1977. A lot the workers such as the electricians and maintenance guys thought the idea a pain and were dead against letting the public in to the 'hallowed' stadium, but I seem to remember Don was all for it! I spent many an hour in his hut in the break yard talking about the pitch and the history of the place. I remember he seemed very proud when he was out inspecting the pitch when the tour guide pointed him out to his party and announced that that man over there is Wembley's head groundsmen. Many on the tours, especially foreigners were awestruck in seeing the head honcho of the most famous sporting ground in the world.

I left Wembley in October 1982 and never saw Don again unfortunately. Thanks for the memory!!

Cheers John Feenstra

20th April 2011 Graham Rigby wrote to Don's younger son Don Gallacher Junior

Hi Don Good to hear from you.

I worked at Wembley from 1980 through to 1988 and ran the Guided Tours from 1983 to 87. I had a lot of time for your father and like to think that we got on well. Looking back, it was probably the best time of my working life and for a few years I practically lived at the stadium taking several tours a day. Your father always seemed to be around – a looming presence looking after 'his pitch'. i always knew what I could get away with Don in terms of encroaching on to the grass and that was ABSOLUTELY NOTHING! But he knew that I knew where the boundaries were, and I never tried to push it so we did get on well.

Don came across as a bit of a bluff Londoner but in many ways he was a bit of a softy, particularly where some of our disabled visitors were concerned. He would throw me a nod occasionally which meant that it was okay for them to get a bit closer to the grass so long as I didn't take advantage! Whenever he was within earshot I would point him out to the visitors as the 'most important man at Wembley – the HEAD GROUNDSMAN! It often seemed as though I had just pointed out the England captain as they certainly appreciated the job he was doing – for much of that period the pitch was in fantastic shape – it had recovered from the ravages of the Horse shows in the early 70's and it was before the pop concerts really kicked in so sitting in the Royal Box at the end of the tour you could really see how good it was.

cont:-

153

He often tried to give the impression that he thought the tours simply got in the way of his work, but Don secretly loved it when someone was brave enough to ask him a question about 'his pitch' and would often carry on the conversation as the group walked around from the players tunnel to the royal tunnel. the more detailed the question the more he liked it! If Don was close by and I asked him a question he would always take the time to answer it addressing himself to the group (I think that he secretly enjoyed that too- I can actually remember a couple of occasions when the tour behind caught us up because your father was answering supplementary questions!).

Without fail he would always talk to me whenever we saw each other and always thought to let me know if the greyhounds or particular bits of machinery were likely to disrupt a tour.

I am not sure that my recollections will be of any use to you as I was a very minor cog in the machine, but it was a good time and I thank you for making me think about it again. Your father often comes to mind when I am watching events at the 'new Wembley' and I wonder what he would have made of the new stadium (to me it is very impressive but you could be in any stadium anywhere in the world - when you were in the old stadium you couldn't have been anywhere else!) and I certainly wonder what he would have made of the state of the pitch and its need to be constantly re-laid.

Good luck with the memoirs and thanks for jogging some memories in me. if i can think of anything else I'll drop you a line.

Kind regards

Graham (Graham RIGNEY.)

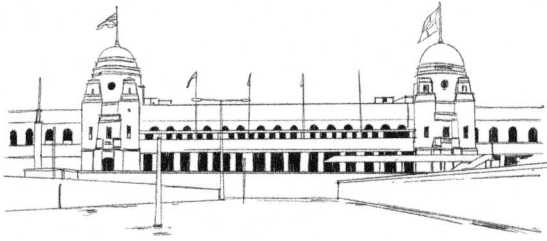

Chapter 11

The Team

Any team that gets to play at Wembley are obviously the best in the country, occasionally the world, working in perfect harmony and playing to carefully calculated strategies that are honed to perfection during hours of training sessions. Of course, they are. But as far as the Wembley playing surface is concerned I reckon that I managed the most important team of the lot; their performance on the famous pitch is not particularly entertaining but the results are no less important, for all that, I'm not suggesting anyone paying to watch them even if they sometimes make me laugh, it's the ground staff and over the years they've been a pretty good gang.

Needless to say, as with every other team, you get the odd bad player, even the occasional nut case deserving of a red card, some are so bad you wonder how they got in the squad in the first place. But my view of the chaps who go to work at any kind of sports ground are that they are either crackers or dedicated and usually a bit of both. They have got to be, the conditions aren't tolerated in any industrial equivalent, that I know of, its hard work with little comfort. Pretty much all of the work that they do is carried out in the open and even in the summer the shadow cast by the stadium shields any sunshine from the ground inside, so very often they either cook, get saturated or freeze and in our climate it is often the latter.

Some jobs are worse than others. The sort of miserable job that comes to mind for example was in the days of the grass greyhound track, when huge tarpaulin sheets were used to cover it a great deal of the time. There were 52 huge sheets, and I worked with the blokes in freezing conditions to get them rolled back in time for a meeting. Often covered in frost and sometimes inches of snow which had to be shovelled off first and I've seen big men almost in tears with the cold. Then at the end of the dog meeting all the sheets had to be put back again, a really miserable job. There were plenty of times that we turfed that track in torrential rain, and although the gang wore waterproof clothing, that didn't alter the fact they were getting very wet on the outside, and because of the material that the clothing is made of and the effort needed for the job, they were sweating from the inside, all the conditions to produce a variety of illnesses, so I appreciated the efforts of my team, even if I am their sole supporter.

Jacky Packham was just out of the navy when he started, Jack was offered a job on Wembley ground staff which he took while he looked around for something more fitting. He was still there 36 years later, still looking I suspect. Quickly becoming the Deputy Head groundsman and a good one. He's seen the lot, from the Olympic Games to the world cup, so many events that they are almost countless. He can tell stories about them until his teeth fall out and one of these days we are going to work out to the nearest 1000 miles, just how far he's walked behind the mower on Wembley's pitch too.

Also, there after thirty years Reg Barwick, who became Groundsman Charge Hand, often the butt of the lads jokes, but a good all-rounder. We have Alan Malzard an Australian who seems to prefer the outback to Wembley and the aggravation that goes it. Amongst other things he became responsible for the mowing of the pitch, few are allowed that task. He has been with us a few years now, and was made Assistant Head Groundsman, he knows his job and can deal with any event that's staged at Wembley. When the Aussies get him back he'll be worth having.

Jim Hawes, a groundsman, and a very useful one at that, he could if he chose, go to a number of places as head groundsman, but he has turned down each offer. I am not sorry because he's an important member of the merry men.

I had two trainees, Peter Smith and Carl Coupar, young enough to learn a lot over the coming years and will do justice to me in time to come; both are willing workers, no matter what they are asked do and that's part of getting it right. This group of workers are a team because they understand each other, understand what I want and what my standards are, and their sense of humour is now nearly as horrible as mine. In a job like this if you didn't let it out on the back of a joke you could end up walking the walls or thumping each other.

We've used a lot of casual staff from time to time and there have been quite a lot of people start and move on, some were good blokes, who are often the hardest to keep. There were also workers who were miseries too, you always get the odd one who thinks a good day out is a game of patience in the cemetery. I have also had staff that do nothing but moan all day, find fault with everything and everybody and if it wasn't for my sense of humour and the more light-hearted lads that make up the gang, we would easily get down to their level and life's just too short for that. Usually, the humour that I talk of is like most jokes, invariably at the expense of someone else, but at our place the joke just as often turns full circle.

Up until 1980 I had casual labour from an agency used mainly for work outside of the arena proper, cutting grass, cleaning flower beds, and trimming trees. I was usually lucky with such staff, for most of the time I had Australian or New Zealand lads, a regular supply of world travellers and on one occasion two Spanish chaps. One of the jobs that come to mind was lopping trees. I had to have the lower branches cut off all the trees in Olympic way so that the public didn't catch their heads. We had used a contractor on occasions but it had taken one man and a lad over a week, so I decided to use casuals. My three lads were issued with appropriate tools, saws, small axes etc; and shown what was wanted. The tallest was told to reach as high as was safe and that would be their guidelines, he was well over 6ft tall, in fact all three were big fellows. They started at 8.15 am and by 3.30 pm the same day came back for another job, I thought they'd got fed up and wanted a change, but they were finished and what's more all the timber was in neat piles for the lorry to collect. I was delighted and asked if they had done anything like it before. Of course, they had, unbeknown to me I'd picked the ideal job for them all three were New Zealand Forestry Rangers on a working holiday in England, brilliant.

We had another young lad, when I first went to Wembley, who seemed to have a knack of doing everything wrong, or at least back to front. He wasn't a ground staff man at all but one of the 'Heavy Gang' and for weeks I thought he was a bit slow, but one night at the 'Dogs' he was caught smoking and my predecessor gave him a right telling off. But typical of the shrewd Irish humour, some thirty minutes later the lad approached Percy and meekly said, 'please sir would it be permissible to suck a toffee', I roared, it was micky taking at its best, not surprisingly Percy didn't see it the same way.

The same lad was lent to me on one occasion, and I put him to work on a 'soil shredder', a machine which you shovel huge clods of soil into on one side and no matter how big or what was in it, it gets milled and screened, resulting in good fine soil flying out of the front. Any stones or other rubbish gets separated and went out the bottom. I explained the principle, gave a little demonstration and left him to it. Three hours later I went back to see how he was getting on and when I saw what he was doing I just stood fascinated. I watched him for about five minutes because he didn't know I was there.

Instead of letting the machine do the work he was breaking every bit of earth up before putting it in, he was knocking himself out smashing the clods with the shovel, jumping up and down on them before putting them through the machine, the poor devil had been doing this for hours. I walked up to him picking a solid lump of earth about twice the size of a football and threw it into the shredder, you know the result, it disappeared completely, it didn't even bounce, it just came out divided into its respective parts, I didn't have the heart to tell him off, he'd worked so hard. My only comment to him was "for God sake, don't tell the others". I didn't think there was more room for jokes about the Irish in this place. That lad was so shy when he first came to Wembley, it took me weeks to get him to talk to anyone, but then when he started we couldn't stop him.

It's not just the Irish who get the mickey taken out of them of course, being like the League of Nations the Aussies and the English have to take it too and you ought to hear how they talk to the occasional Italian. Every word ending in 'a' such as 'getta yourself, over 'eera' and so on;

Another character who worked in the 'Heavy Gang' was 'Big Fred' I can't remember his second name, but nobody had to, everyone know who Big Fred was. He was built like a Giant, and we always put his strength to good use. Such as the day my office had to be moved. It's an office in name only, it's actually a big wooden hut, the type that a General Foreman uses on a building site. One day another 'expert', of which we have many, decided that the window and door were facing the wrong way. It hadn't bothered me up to then, nor presumably my predecessors. But I'm an amenable sort of bloke and went along with it. As in 'who cares?'. A stadium engineer appeared one day and suggested that we had the carpenters cut out new holes for the window and door, and board up the holes left behind. A simple solution to him, although not to those of the team, overhearing yet another management gem, it hadn't occurred to him that being portable we could lift it up and turn the whole thing right around.

Anyway, as soon as he'd gone and regardless of the list of jobs lined up, we sent some lads to find some tubular scaffold poles to put under it to roll the hut into its new position, but they had a problem getting the pipes under to start it off, and they couldn't get hold of it properly to lift. Then 'Big Fred' arrived, took a glance, 'tutted' dramatically and said, 'stand back'. He stood in the doorway of the hut, feet outside, hands stretched up holding the top of the door frame and when he was comfortable he said to the blokes', 'Get ready with the poles, I'll lift it for you'. We still thought he was joking especially as half a dozen blokes had already tried to move it the few inches that we needed. But he wasn't joking, and while one of the gang stood by with a scaffold pole,

Fred just straightened his arms out and the hut went up, not a drop of sweat on his brow. It was so hard to believe it happened that way that we checked it after he'd gone. We looked at how he had stood with his feet outside, arms outstretched, it meant he was leaning backwards lifting a weight some six men couldn't move. He was very handy our Fred, we turned the hut round very easily after that, I was very grateful. I dread to think how long it would have taken without him. We didn't think much more about it until a week later when the carpenters turned up to cut and replace the new door and window. Needless to say, no-one enlightened them as they looked over the hut and to their instructions, and wandered off muttering about armchair planners.

Fred performed great feats of strength during his working days at Wembley, but unfortunately was sacked in an argument about pay and conditions for the heavy gang. From what I can gather others used him and his size and encouraged him to be a spokesman on their behalf but it got out of hand. So 'Big Fred' went, and the others remained. Next time I need my doors and windows moved I'll just have to do it their way and cut new one's out and board up the empty holes. Even though the so-called benefits of the change remained a mystery.

Another big chap joined the staff, and I was very pleased with him too, he was big and had tremendous strength, his name was Alfie Kendall and had plenty of heavy work put onto him.

His least obvious but none the less outstanding feat of strength in my book was carrying a tray of 24 plants in pots (clay not plastic) from the Royal Tunnel across to my office on the opposite side of the stadium, you try it. The lads saw him take the tray with outstretched arms, turned around and walked out of the Royal Tunnel, stepped over the greyhound track fence, crossed the shale path, over the greyhound fence again, then the greyhound track, over the wall, up the terrace steps, down the stone steps, onto the levels to my office, kicked at the door because his arms were full and when I answered the door he still had his arms stretched out in front of his body, he hadn't put them down once, that's what I call strength.

He left us flabbergasted on another day too it was just after five o'clock. I decided to water the pitch all evening, I suddenly missed big Alf, I was furious as I thought he had cleared off early. Then I heard him shout from the South Terrace. 'Tea Up'. Then he did a repeat of his strong man act only not with plants this time it was a similarly huge tray with milk, sugar, mugs and a ruddy great teapot. His arms were outstretched as though he was holding a spool of knitting wool. He planted the tray down in the middle of the pitch as though he was setting a picnic, offered to 'be mum' and proceeded to pour everyone tea. Fortunately, no one took a photo of our picnic on the sacred turf, so much for rules.

It wasn't long after that we lost Big Alfie when he went off to join the circus. Not really, the job was erecting exhibition stands but we liked to think he was doing strong man acts under a big top, it suited our image of him better, he was a great worker and yet another character in a long list of characters.

It's not all problems at Wembley we do have lighter moments and occasionally a lot of laughs. They say that in the face of adversity put up two fingers and turn it into humour, sometimes the joke is on you, sometimes not. It's the British way you know.

We had a massive site clearance job at the back of the stadium one time and a contractor turned up with several trucks carrying plant, machinery and equipment. My lads were out there generally being nosey, including myself and our George McElroy.

Now George absolutely loved animals and he'd spotted a little white dog sitting in one of the vans and he did what came naturally to him by going up to the open window to make a fuss of it. Poor George, he never saw it coming, most of us had realised it was a Jack Russell terrier and as one of the lads shouted a warning, the 'cute' little dog lunged at George and bit him on the nose. If that wasn't bad enough, the little tyke held on to it. Fortunately, the owner was nearby and managed to force its mouth apart sufficient to release George's 'hooter'. Needless to say, there was a mixture of sympathy and hysterical laughter, more the latter than the former, especially from his so called mates. But his nose was in a state and serious enough for hospital treatment and despite the obvious pain and discomfort it didn't stop the lads ribbing him talking of needing a rabies injection, which in turn, started the dog owner off regarding it as an insult to his dog and so it went around. That story went on for weeks, being elaborated on with each telling of the tale of the tiny dog that got George by the nose. Not helped of course by the huge bandage.

Another chap, Jerry Warren was driving the tractor one day when for whatever reason and heaven knows how, it tipped over trapping his foot quite badly. Anyway, we got him free, put him in my car and I took him to the hospital, where, convinced it was broken I left him in the casualty department and told him to telephone the office when they had got him sorted and someone would pick him up. I got back in my car thinking poor old Jerry would be off work for a few weeks and made my way back to the stadium, where I was met by? Jerry Warren. I couldn't believe my eyes, looked at him, looked at my watch and honestly thought I had gone potty. His explanation? He haf decided that he didn't need treatment, could limp along without too much pain and followed me out of casualty but not quite quick enough to attract my attention. He'd spotted a minicab dropping someone off at the door and jumped in to take him back to work. I still couldn't figure out how they beat me back to Wembley, that minicab must have been jet propelled. So that story was added to the lads' repertoire, of gags that tended to revolve around my 'slow' car and me being 'a bit of a steady driver'.

Talking of tractors, one of the most hilarious sights I have seen at Wembley was the day a tractor driver, an 'outsider' who was rather new to the place, drove down the Brake Yard Tunnel at a fair pace and oblivious to, or simply choosing to ignore the ground staff shouting at him to stop, just kept going. You know the type 'don't tell me how to drive'. By the time he realised what they were shouting about, the noise of the tractor jamming itself under the low roof of the tunnel and more significantly the pipes crossing the low roof of the tunnel, sort of did the job for him.

Fortunately, nothing was seriously damaged, well nothing more important than this bloke's ego, which was torn to shreds by my lot asking him a range of questions relating to his eyesight, hearing, ability to drive etc; The poor devil had to sit there taking it for what must have seemed an eternity, as they got the tools out and dismantled the tractor as efficiently as they extricated the mickey out of the hapless driver. What he didn't know was that they knew what tools they needed and what to do because it wasn't the first time it had happened, and it hadn't only been done by 'an outsider'. But then it did us all a power of good to watch someone else make a clot of himself for a change.

George, whose exploits with his nose and the Jack Russell dog mentioned previously had a habit of staggering from time to time.

He described it as 'dizzy spells' but no-one knew what they were caused by. Anyway, one day I walked onto the pitch and noticed my assistant groundsman Jacky Packham staggering about at the other end of the ground. Jacky was a notorious joker so at first I took no notice, believing that he was taking the mickey out of George. But then I realised that he didn't have an audience and George wasn't around, something was very wrong. I ran down the pitch (not my favourite pastime) and saw that Jacky was bleeding from the forehead and was clearly stunned. At first he couldn't explain what had happened, how could he bang his head pushing a line marker at the edge of the pitch. I got him to sit down and looked around, even looked up as though something had fallen from the sky and still it didn't make any sense how he had been hurt. Others arrived, someone got the first aid kit and we sorted Jacky out. Then with his help eventually figured out what had happened.

He had been marking out the pitch which takes care and precision and we do that by using nylon range lines with steel pins at each end. The lines are pulled as tight as possible to ensure a good straight line and obviously secure it by pushing the pins into the ground. We think what had happened was that one of the lads had accidentally kicked or tripped on the line near to a pin but miles from Jacky and didn't twig the implications and carried on to wherever he was off to in the first place. But the pin came out of the ground and the line being like a stretched elastic band catapulted the pin though the air like a rocket, direct to the opposite pin which in this case was blocked by Jacky's head. Freak accident, yes of course and he could have been killed or blinded, so we thought we were lucky that day and learned yet another lesson. He got quite a livid scar as a result and used it occasionally to make the point that accidents can happen on a quiet sunny day in the middle of a football pitch, with nothing around but a white line marker and a bit of string. On the other hand, it could only happen to our Jacky and only at Wembley.

It should be said that health & safety is a big issue and taken very seriously and the gang doesn't need to be heavily regulated to use common sense and or take advice when dished out. But with our lot, rules for the sake of having a rule leave themselves open for misinterpretation and sometimes regarded as fair game. One such rule applied when our people who were engaged in the greyhound meetings. Simple enough, staff in or around the track were alerted by an official ringing a bell when the stuffed hare was about to be released. Known unofficially as the 'ding-ding' watch, hardly life threatening, but a sensible requirement nonetheless.

To signal the start of a race, actually when the hare moves off (not on its own, a bell was rung as a signal, quite a noisy bell, in fact a very noisy bell. Nothing sophisticated, just a man who stood at the brake (where the hare is pulled up, and on this occasion it was our Reg who had to ring the bell. Unfortunately, his mind must have been elsewhere because he forgot and eventually remembered when the hare had gone and travelled about halfway along the track straight. Serious? Of course, it was, but I doubt if many people knew it had happened or as no-one was on the track, cared for that matter. The dogs leapt out after the hare as it flashed by them, it didn't affect the race, therefore no-one could have lost money or have cause for complaint. It's a bell, which is normally rung, and it wasn't. At this point it would be causing a bit of mickey taking at Reg's expense.

Except for one steward who phoned me, playing hell about my stupid staff, he went off alarming. To him every rule in the book

166

had been broken. What rubbish! Nevertheless, reluctant as I was, I had no option but to reprimand the wrongdoer, even though it was an 'accident', or at worst an aberration. Needless to say, Reg got his own back, during the very next race meeting.

The hare left the brake, Reg rang the bell and rang the bell and kept the bell ringing until the dogs left the traps three bends away. That got everyone's attention, it's a wonder the fire brigade didn't turn out or the greyhounds run out of the stadium in sheer fright. What a noise! Except that is from the 'jobs-worth' steward, nor anyone else for that matter, and coincidentally, the bell vanished completely soon after and was out of use for a long time. No longer vital to the races it would seem.

It makes a good story though, usually told by someone not even there and with each telling it gets more exaggerated and graphic to visualise Reg thumping that bell for all its worth. It makes for a good laugh when the lads are a bit low, even better when it's at the expense of 'the system'.

A few years ago, we had a lad who also tried too hard, ever eager to please, and to protect the seemingly innocent, let's say his name was Bob. One day he was given the task of aerating the pitch using a motorised spiker, can't go wrong, short of putting a dozen holes in his foot, it was the perfect task for his skill set. It needed doing and after an hour so did he, because as well as putting a million or so holes in the pitch, he managed to do the same to six water hoses that had been stretched across the turf and shouldn't have been too difficult to spot, especially when all around him, beautiful fountains were springing up from all our hosepipes.

There were those that said that it must have been deliberate as no-one could be that silly. But having experienced more incidents like that than I could have imagined possible, I just didn't know anymore and that one went into the annals of stories that end up with 'he did what?'

Still, it's nice to come across a gang who take their work seriously for the most part but are able to see the funnier side of life when it gets a bit beyond a joke, even more so when the joke is on themselves. That's what I had been fortunate enough to keep together, a good team who know when to pull out the stops when the chips were down but laugh at each other when they are up to their knees in the mire.

So next time the teams come out of the players tunnel to the roar of the crowd with much pomp and splendour. Keep your eye out for the groundsman's team, they will be the ones on the side-lines, sometimes leaning on a fork, usually with muddy knees waiting to leap into action when needed. But actually, they're waiting for everyone to bugger off so they can clean up and go home.

Groundstaff at Royal Tunnel May 83

Photos: Don with Jack Packham
and some of the team

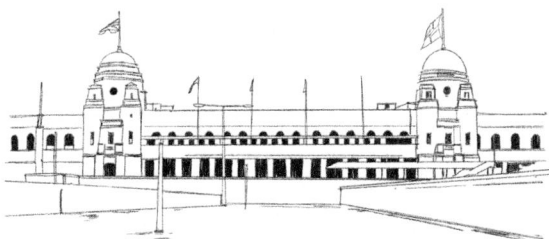

Chapter 12

An American Invasion

Many months before they landed, there was talk of staging American Football at Wembley including a story that Tottenham Hotspur Football Club was going to sponsor the whole thing. But although it seemed a great idea it was presumed to be just talk and as far as I was concerned, Wembley is in the business of staging events and we had heard such ideas before. Then one day the boss came out onto the pitch (yes it was allowed, he was the boss) and said very enthusiastically that he was 99% sure that somebody was going to put the show on. Funny how that description was often used, not a game or a match, it was to be a 'show'. How right they were. The plan became a pre-season match between The Minnesota Vikings and The St Louis Cardinals in August 1983.

Anyway, in due course we started to see odd groups or American visitors walking around with our management and on a couple of occasions I was called into the talks about setting up the pitch. I told them that I could mark out any type of pitch providing that I had the plan of the field. My word you should have seen the schematic drawing. Not long afterward when it became positive that a match was going to take place, I met the man with the latest delegation of Americans who was going to show us how they wanted the ground marked out. His name was Sam Monson who was responsible for the football grounds of the Minnesota Vikings and obviously well acquainted with the layout of American Football pitches. Sam proved to be an excellent tutor and got on well with my staff as well as myself. In fact, he turned out to be 'just one of the boys' happy to muck in with everybody, had a drink with the ground staff in the club at lunch time and generally made it clear that he was not just full of wind and really did know his trade.

The marking of an American Football field was certainly different with end zones, numerals and centre markings, not to mention pylons and strange goals and it took lots more whiting than soccer or rugby, not just because there are many more lines, but some of them had to be double or treble width. The antenna type goalposts were made in England which was handy and reminded me that Wembley had hosted American Football many years previously and had not long discarded the posts, although they were more rugby type. Many more pieces of kit were shipped over from the 'States' such as stencils for the large numbers that mark the yards on the 'Grid' and the American National Football (NFL) emblem, a very large badge which was painted in the centre of the pitch, red, white and blue. We used coloured dyes for that and after the match the white and the blue washed out quite easily. But even with high pressure washers we failed to get the red dye out and finally resorted to re-turfing any areas that had been marked red.

A good deal of work and planning went into the preparation and setting up of the pitch, much of which was new to most of us. So, for once we were going by plans, drawings plus guidance from Sam rather than our instinct and experience. It included very careful measurement and placement of markings, erecting the posts and pylons and of course the usual mowing to ensure the Wembley turf showed through all of the 'make up'. But on the Friday before the big game, we were putting the finishing touches to everything and I spent what seemed to be a good deal of the day being interviewed by American TV and radio crews who managed to talk about six times faster than I could, which is saying something. It was, dare I say, a fairly relaxed atmosphere and at a point a murmur of excitement ran around the ground, particularly with the media people as we were about to witness the entry of the gladiators. I, with others, looked toward the players tunnel and was speechless, never in my life had I seen so many large men all together and I have seen plenty. These men were giants, well over six feet tall and around eighteen stone on average, although some must have been a lot more. A lot of them had their padding on but even the men without the body armour were huge and to my amazement they could run like greyhounds as they practiced short sprints across the turf. Most of them seemed impressed with the pitch and said some nice things about it referring to it as 'The real grass'.

Having only ever seen American Football on TV or old films I was intrigued by the uniforms, particularly the footwear, a sort of cross between a football boot and a basketball boot with bits sticking out. The first chap I asked about them was reluctant to tell me or maybe he just didn't understand my accent. But Sam told him that I was the man in charge of the turf, which brought collective interest and cooperation from all the Minnesota players.

One of the media blokes latched on to this and interviewed me again about the damage we expect from these boots, some of which had extensions on the sole protruding out from the front about three eighths of an inch. These were for the goal kickers, a specialist job of course and my mind drifted to my youth when I had a reputation as a kicker with both feet of soccer balls (not so common today) and wondered how much I would have earned in America. When I played, football wages were very poor, clearly it had always been different in American Football. The Minnesota team did have an English player, a successful goal kicker in the States and I had quite a long chat with him finding out that he had played in League Football just two years before.

Sam Monson pointed out to me where the damage to the turf, if any would be done and I was quite happy to take his word for it, he had been right about everything else he had told us. What we had not reckoned on was a pitch invasion, it was not a big crowd but they managed to do a lot of damage following the match. But the main damage was something else we hadn't bargained for and wiped out a large strip of new turf that had been laid a few weeks previously. Not on the pitch but along the sides.

The teams comprised 45 players per team, but only 11 each side are on the playing area at any time during the game, the rest were standing right along the south side of the pitch in what was called the 'team area', to the rear of the 'coach box'. Such an innocent sounding space until on match day when it's filled with 60 odd 'giants' kitted and booted, plus umpires, coaches, trainers and a variety of officials all jumping up and down like mad. It doesn't need a wild imagination to realize what the turf looked like when the game was over, we have had teams of horses on the turf that did less damage.

It has often been said that you shouldn't judge a book by its cover and that became clear to me when I got into a conversation with an elderly gentleman who was just walking around the pitch seemingly taking it all in along with the other American visitors. He did seem a little out of place, partly because of his suit and clothes which were a bit dated and heavy for the August weather. But we chatted and I answered the questions that he put to me about the stadium and events that we held there, typical of my response to someone on a guided tour. Afterwards, he wandered off and a media type asked me what the gentleman (I can't remember his name) had been talking to me about, which I thought was a bit nosy even for a TV man. It turned out that the old gentleman owned one of the teams and was a dollar millionaire many times over, so much for appearances.

I was interviewed by several US sports TV channels and four or five radio stations, apparently due to the interest by American fans, demonstrated by the keenness of the people who had flown over to witness what was to be the first match played by American Pro teams in Europe. After a while LBC radio and the BBC joined in the fun and I must say that I lapped it up. It isn't often that a groundsman is the focus of attention, most are kept in the background, but these people were going to town in a big way. It must be an American thing and over the days I had some serious offers to go to the States to talk on turf and about Wembley Stadium in general. But I didn't take it up, I doubted that the bosses would be keen, and my wife was a poor traveller and I wouldn't go on my own. But I remained in touch and gave advice when asked, for several years, but at a distance.

The game was indeed a spectacle at least for the uninitiated like me and I thought it a great pity that there wasn't a much larger crowd, about 30,000 I believe, which is very low by Wembley standards. It was a mixture of US Visitors, ex pats, British fans of

American football and the inquisitive. Those that did come were mostly placed in the lower tiers of seats which I think was a mistake, I had the impression that it is a game that should be seen from higher up in the stands rather than pitch level. The experts told me that it's best watched from above, as it is played like a huge game of chess with human pieces which I understand was a fair analogy. Sam Monson told when a kick is to take place, so many men leave the pitch, and the specialist kicker comes on with his mates almost like labourers. There are several coaches in the stands, as well as pitch side, equipped with radios feeding information about the run of play and constantly changing players on the field. It really is nothing like football (soccer) or rugby or for that matter anything else I had witnessed. It really was spectacular and according to the scoreboard the Vikings won 28-10 otherwise I wouldn't have had a clue what was going on.

Shame about the state of the turf in the team area, but not to worry, we had a couple of weeks to go before the Charity Shield was to be played!

So began the long running association between American Football and Wembley Stadium, I wasn't available when they came to town in 1984, being seriously ill. But I remember the boss phoning me at home to ask if my own staff were capable of setting out the pitch without a great deal of help from the American specialists. There must have been some talk of a gang coming over if necessary. I told him that I was 100% positive our blokes could produce a perfect set up for the day and Dons team did me and Wembley Stadium proud. It went very well and continues to this day and on into the new generations.

Marking out an American Football pitch had unique
challenges, but great fun.

The main damage was something else we hadn't bargained for as
it wasn't on the pitch, but in the very crowded 'team' area

,

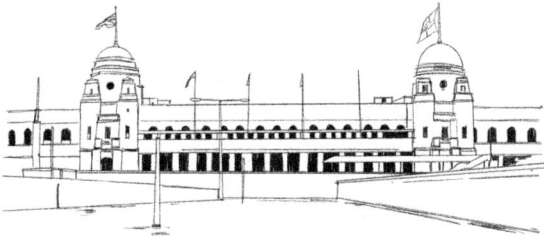

Chapter 13

Who Needs Practice?

The annual concentration of 'Finals' makes the period between March and June just about the busiest in the Wembley calendar, but the Spring of '81' really got out of hand. What with the poor weather, the cutbacks on staff and practice matches it was the closest I'd been to walking out on Wembley with no regrets at all.

It began in earnest with my first big game of the year on March 14th, the League Cup Final and on that occasion it was between Liverpool and West Ham, a good game to start my busy season and not a bad one to end Liverpool's because although the game ended in a draw 1-1 they went on to win in the replay. The following week was devoted to changing the pitch from football to hockey to accommodate the Women's Hockey International, England versus Wales, which was to be played on the Saturday to a packed crowd, with Queen Elizabeth in attendance. The women's hockey match is always an enjoyable day for me as the crowd seem to be there for a good day out, just as competitive as any other sport but seemingly less tribal. My wife says that it's actually because I like the idea of females outnumbering the males (including me) by about 500 to one, perish the thought, I doubt I was ever in danger.

The Womens Hockey Team rarely had time to practice even though they sometimes claimed that the grass was too long for their high-speed sport. But the day after the hockey match was spent repairing the pitch, replacing torn out turf and filling in holes. My word those hockey sticks play havoc with the playing surface, but still it was just the usual routine. What I didn't like much was the incessant rain which, throughout that period, had become just as routine and on that Sunday it was particularly bad, so much so that despite the weatherproofs we all had to have a change of clothes during the day, and we still went home soaked. But by Monday afternoon when the ground staff had to get the traps ready for greyhound racing, the pitch was two thirds done and was starting to look good again. On Tuesday morning and in defiance of the weather we marked out the lines for football again, because on Wednesday night, 25th March, England would play Spain in a friendly match. But first, they would 'need some practice'.

Now the idea of a squad of international footballers needing to practice on the pitch the day before the match seems a bit far-fetched to me. If it isn't necessary for league matches at home or abroad, why for a 'friendly' international game. Getting the feel of the pitch I can understand and that was the original motive for visiting teams, but that only needs a kick about in training shoes on most grounds and usually happens half an hour or so before the kick-off. Practicing set pieces, penalty kicks and corners on any pitch 24 hours before the real thing has little to do with getting 'acclimatized' to the ground. Particularly not for international players and in my book it's a dead liberty because that sort of coaching should have been (would have been) done on a training ground, not on England's finest. Test Cricketers don't knock up on the wickets of Lords and Headingly the night before a test match, tennis players aren't allowed to let rip on the centre court at Wimbledon. So why should they do it on my pitch, particularly on a rainy day. However, it's become something of a 'right' and happens all over the world to a greater or lesser degree and as a rule I'm not bothered because the Wembley surface can usually take it. But on this occasion the surface had been carved up two weeks in a row and the wet conditions meant that any damage done in a practice game wouldn't leave enough time to make the pitch look or play as well as it ought to for an important International Match.

So, on the Tuesday before the big game I advised the stadium manager about my concern and asked that the FA be approached to have the traditional practice match planned for that night, cancelled. Perhaps find an alternative ground in the area. I got a straightforward and immediate answer, not from the FA, but from the stadium manager, 'No'.

That evening the Spanish squad arrived 'to get the feel of the ground'. They got the feel of it all right, it had been pouring with rain all the afternoon and evening even while they were 'practicing' it's a wonder they didn't catch pneumonia. The next day, the morning of the match, my apprehension for what damage may have been done was dispelled for a while. As I walked onto the pitch from the Break-yard Tunnel I could see no damage at all at that end. Great, I thought, they must have cancelled it after all. Did they hell as like. By the time I got to the halfway line I could see that somebody had been on my pitch and from the way it looked I thought it must have been the Household Cavalry having a bit of a practice with a team of horses complete with guncarriage. Apparently, in an effort to cause as little damage as possible the Spaniards had been asked to confine their practice to one end of the ground in the penalty area and the corners. Unfortunately, that only made matters worse and from the terraces I could see that I had a pitch that was two thirds perfect playing surface, all striped shades of green and smooth as a snooker table. But one third, pock-marked, muddy brown, badly cut up and torn. With the real game due to kick-off at 7.45 that night, we had our work cut out to repair and make good again and by good, I mean seriously average.

Perhaps they had the right idea though and the FA /stadium manager may have slipped up because the Spanish beat England 2 goals to 1, perhaps England should have 'practiced' at the other end to balance it out.

Thursday and Friday went by repairing and preparing again for yet another international football match due on Saturday, a schoolboy match this time, but just as important as any other. This was the England against Northern Ireland game and fortunately the weather backed off long enough to give them a good playing surface, one that did justice to the event. So, with four major events and a practice match in 14 days behind us, we set about replacing divots, filling in holes and making the Wembley pitch live up to the glossy pictures in the programmes. What the players would make of it was another matter.

This was followed by a few weeks respite before the fifth big game in the calendar during which time I had more than a few run-ins with the stadium management. This was because during this intense period, their idea of priorities was seldom mine and with my ground staff reduced along with every other department plus a rigidly enforced ruling on overtime, we clashed again and again. Well, I knew we had to cut back, the ground staff even realised it, unfortunately the grass, moss and other weeds just kept on growing at the weekends, it seemed that nature didn't realise that there was a recession on.

For example, the day before the FA Vase Final, my ground staff were directed off of a job I'd given them on the pitch, to attend to the roses outside the conference centre. That's all right as that's my province too and in normal circumstances would have received my utmost attention. But not at the expense of the big green patch inside the stadium, that's where the games were being played, not amid the blooms in the blooming car park.

Saturday 25th April the FA Vase Final, not a big gate for this game but just as many players on the pitch and they probably cover more ground than the average first division teams, so Sunday was repair and put right.

Guess what? The Romanians were playing on Wednesday, so they had to have a practice match, I didn't bother to ask for it to be cancelled there was no point. England played Romania in a qualifying match for the World Cup on a some¬what spotty Wembley. It was another evening game as most mid–week matches were with kick off at 7.45 pm and although it had been a long day, our work had to start again when the match finished. As the players were still going down the tunnel, we were removing nets and goal posts and washing out the soccer lines, because in three days' time, the Rugby League Challenge Final would kick off, that gave us two whole days to get the pitch ready for them. Whoopee! As it happens the rugby players probably didn't give a 'monkeys' about the surface but I did.

Thursday was spent attending to the previous night's scars and there were plenty of them. Usually, the rugby posts go up by the Thursday before the game but there was no time and no spare men so they didn't get erected until Friday morning which put everything else behind. It makes sense to mark the pitch before the rugby posts are erected but this time we just couldn't do it.

The 45ft long posts are the heaviest I've ever come across and on this occasion that wasn't appreciated very much. The sockets were far bigger than the base of these posts and the operation took longer than it should, but isn't that always the way when you are having a good time and we still hadn't started marking the lines for Rugby. At one time that Friday morning, the posts were still being aligned while the lines were being marked, while Alan was mowing the pitch and another tradition was about to happen. The inspection of the pitch by the visitors.

For any of the big games, which in the case of Wembley means most of them, it's tradition for the opposing teams to turn up on the day before for a walkabout. Some managers regard it as an important part of the players pre-match preparation, it supposedly gets them used to the place. Actually, an empty stadium is nothing like the same as the one they'll enter on the day of the match but they can examine the pitch carefully and sometimes they quiz me about different things. It's usually very light and good fun. Very often the team managers and coaches have been there nearly as often as I have, and they sometimes stop and chat for a while too.

The rugby visitors have a different slant on getting a feel of the pitch, what they sometimes do the afternoon before their big match is to have a run out on the pitch in track suits and training shoes and on this occasion, even that didn't seem like a good idea to me but I was a bit preoccupied to do much about it and promptly forgot to comment.

About lunchtime, the Widnes team trooped onto the pitch wearing track suits and boots, not training shoes and throwing rugby balls about and although they were expected, the suddenness of their arrival took me aback as we weren't ready for that style of inspection. On top of that, the school teams who were also playing on the Saturday arrived along with the ball boys and they too ran out onto the pitch, balls and all, and nobody seemed to be in charge of them. It wasn't the lads' fault; doubtless someone had indicated to them that it was all right to have a gallop over the Wembley pitch. Who wouldn't, given the opportunity? But nobody stepped forward and said 'It was me' and the Stadium bods who should have been responsible for this bit of public relations were nowhere to be found.

What with mowing, marking and repairs going on with players of all shapes and sizes running around, even to the point where they were tripping over the string that we were using to mark out the lines, I called a halt to the activities of my blokes. It was no good carrying on, no individual listened to my pleading and no one in authority chose to be around to do it for me. So, I called the ground staff off, sent them to another job and watched the rugby players as they stepped onto the newly marked white lines to make pretty footprints all over the lush green turf. Eventually teachers arrived bringing some semblance of order to the youngsters. But a walkabout of ten minutes had become over an hour and a very lively hour at that, and I still had the other team to come yet. I went off for a tea break and hoped that someone would have the sense to handle Hull Kingston Rovers, the other team visitors who were due to arrive any minute.

I hadn't been in my office more than a few minutes when I got a telephone call from the Stadium Engineer to say that the pitch was obviously not ready and there was nobody working on it. Well, I didn't know whether to laugh or cry so I blew my top, I think we both slammed the phone down on each other.

As it turned out Hull Kingston Rovers arrived, walked over the pitch and went away again. The rest of the afternoon was spent marking out the final lines, clearing away, and getting shaped up for a greyhound meeting, Friday night being dogs' night, regardless of Cup Finals.

Saturday 2nd May was dry and bright and looked as though it would stay so for the whole day. By the time I reached Wembley, fans were already there, they never cease to amaze me when they go to the lengths that they do to follow their teams. Some of these people are found sleeping in their cars in the car park, some sleep on the steps outside. It's not as though they have to queue up for a ticket for these matches, yet there they were shouting and waving their banners, a good eight hours before the kick off.

As it happens the Rugby League fans are generally a good humoured and well-behaved crowd. There's rarely any trouble among them and I share the theory, that most of their pushing, kicking and thumping is done for them by the players on the park. It's certainly true that for a bunch of hard men, they put most of the football fans to shame when it comes to community singing. On that occasion, the comedians Cannon and Ball were on top of the high rostrum to conduct the 100,000 voices and although it must be a daunting task they had the best crowd to do it with. No filth from the opposing choirs, no pathetically obscene songs to slang each other, just straight song sheet stuff. That's something that rarely happens nowadays but when it does it is a truly amazing sound. A hundred thousand voices singing 'Abide with me' in that stadium will bring a tear to the eye of most of us, and 'The National Anthem' is almost sung with reverence. I couldn't help but stop what I was doing and join in with gusto, I love it.

186

The big match procedure was much the same as usual although with the schoolboys playing before the big game and the presentation of trophies going on, things did get a little bit tight, but all in all, it wasn't a bad day's sport.

By the time that the match was over and despite the celebrations continuing on and off the pitch, we started washing away the rugby lines again. We wouldn't need them for another year and the FA Cup Final between Tottenham Hotspur and Manchester City, was the next match scheduled for the following Saturday and confusing lines had to be thoroughly eradicated.

With the stadium cleared of players and public, the huge rugby posts could be removed, actually lifted up by brute force, but steadied and lowered by a Hy-Mac, then six men carry them off to the storage racks. Followed by crossbars, wedges and all the rugby paraphernalia, not to be seen again for twelve months. A steel plate is put over the post sockets; then soil and finally the same turves that had been cut out the day before topped them off, because the post holes, are inside the area of the football pitch, so they have to be completely and perfectly lost. In fact, it's quite amusing sometimes, seeing the experts with their tape measures trying to find them each year. There are some of us who wait until the smart boys aren't around, who can pace out from a known point and with a spike can locate a socket in minutes, but we don't bother to tell them how it's done. Silly, isn't it?

The week before the FA Cup Final was a hard slog for the ground staff trying to get the pitch up to the standards I demand of them. But on Tuesday it was ready to be cut long ways and by Thursday, when Alan cut it across ways, it was starting to look good again.

Still, the best men that I had, were being re-directed to other tasks around the complex by Wembley managers, still, I fought to keep them on the pitch. Reducing 'unnecessary labour' is great on paper but in this business the demand on time and skills has 'peaks' and something always suffers. That Saturday was to be the 100th FA Cup Final, a very special occasion with the usual 100,000 crowd and a television audience in the tens of millions and the day before the game someone was informing me how many men I needed for the pitch. It would make a bloody Saint swear, and I'm no Saint.

On the afternoon before the big day, the two teams came to look the pitch over and although it wasn't as good as I would have liked for such a special occasion. From a playing point of view, it was a pretty good surface, at least that's what the visitors said to me. With all the rain we'd had over the previous few months, these lads were sometimes playing twice a week on grounds all over the country. Grounds that had taken 3 times as much pounding as mine and to see any grass at all was something of a novelty, so to most of them it looked good. Unfortunately to the powers that be it's supposed to look as though no-one's been near it since last year and they don't help to keep it that way, but that wasn't going to spoil my afternoon not with so many appreciative smiles of approval all around and just to harp on a point, these players were among the best in the world, their comments good or bad are what matter to me and it was nice that they were pleased with what they were going to perform on the next day.

Now I know I keep on saying I'm not biased toward one team or another. but I was born about 100 yards and in sight of the Spurs stadium. My dad played for them and the family were obviously strong supporters. The Paxton Road East Stand dominated every working day of my life when I had the sports ground next door to take care of. Only a wire fence separated the Tottenham pitch from all my rugby and cricket pitches and Henry Naylor, the Spurs groundsman for many years, was a very dear friend and confidante. In the early days some of the greatest Spurs players had training sessions on our college ground and on one occasion, a load of them marched into our back kitchen which backed onto the ground for a tea break. We have a connection, so how can I say with a straight face that I'm not biased?

I'll ignore for a minute the fact that the Spurs fans regularly throw rubbish over my front garden wall and block up all the streets so I can't park near my house when they play at home. But that's the price of living near any football ground, on this occasion I couldn't help but feel an extra part of the goings on, a touch of local pride.

The manager's and players of both teams had a good look around, many of the players were internationals and most of them had been to Wembley before. I couldn't help but watch the faces of the two Argentinians, Ricky Villa and Ossie Ardiles, as they skipped around the pitch, they were genuinely thrilled to be playing in what is probably the most famous football match in the world, its lovely to see players of their calibre as excited as the schoolboys had been a few weeks previously.

I met another old friend that afternoon, the former Spurs Manager, Bill Nicholson and had a chance to chat for quite a while. I first knew Bill in 1938 and his lovely wife Darkie even longer, the Gallacher family home in Trulock Road was a stone's throw from Bills house so we grew up as neighbours and friend for as long as I can remember.

It was a smashing afternoon in every sense, and everything was as ready as I could make it. With a free hand it could easily have been very near to perfect, which is how it should have been. But for the 100th FA Cup Final, that would take £1,000,000 and break the record for gate receipts, I was scratching around looking for blokes to clean up the sand 'D's and didn't have anybody spare.

Cup Final morning was much the same as any other big match day for me, usually if a London side is involved at Wembley the crowds don't bother to get there too early because they don't have too far to travel. But when I got there at 7.00 am, there were already thousands of Spurs and Manchester supporters waiting, all in good humour and good voice.

The year of the cockerel was right, and they'd all got up at dawn crowing for all their worth. The rain that morning, (yes it rained again), didn't bother the supporters at all, it didn't worry me too much either, with this atmosphere, the players feet would hardly touch the ground anyway.

There was a bit of concern about the rain getting the Royals wet and arrangements were made to protect the Queen Mum from the weather, if it persisted, when she went out to meet the players and officials. Fat chance, when the time came she was out there chatting, stepping off the carpet into the wet, dodging from under the umbrellas to talk to someone she'd missed. She must have got soaked and still she smiled. She puts so many of us to shame, no wonder she is thought so highly of.

Prior to that though, the two teams in their smart Cup Final suits walked out onto the pitch to the roars of the delighted fans, I thought to myself, it's a bit of different atmosphere to yesterday lads when a gentle cough echoed around the stadium walls. What a good build up there was too, as a tribute to the 100th anniversary of the FA Cup they presented teams and players representing cup finals of the past, many great names of yesteryear were introduced to the crowds who appeared to be so happy they'd have cheered anything at all, and they did.

They were a lovely crowd that day. For all my criticisms of spectator behaviour and obscenities that have become the norm for football crowds lately. This goodhearted lot were quite the opposite, both Manchester City and Tottenham fans stopped their chanting to sing 'Abide with me' and 'The National Anthem'. In fact, I got the distinct impression there was a special effort from both sides to make it the great spectacle that it became. In fact, the only thing wrong with it was the match itself, that was a bit of a bore unfortunately and that's not just my opinion. I wouldn't make remarks like that unless I was among the majority, in fact you may have noticed that I don't even describe the games that are played here, I'd rather leave that to those who know how to report such things.

No, it was like so many games that fall short of what they are built up to be by the media. The efforts, skills and mistakes were so evenly matched that they virtually cancelled each other out. It wasn't a bad game so much as a disappointing game and when the full-time whistle blew, they were drawing 1-1. Only then did it occur to me that if neither team broke the deadlock in extra time, there would have to be a replay and it might just be here. The teams changed ends and tried to muster up the willpower to play another thirty minutes of extra time. They may not have played their best football, but those poor players had played their hearts out and the frustration that was now showing in some of the tackles was only making matters worse. One thing I did think about was seeing one or two players rolling about the pitch apparently with cramp, something that hadn't happened there for a very long time.

In the dying minutes the crowd tried to raise their respective teams to pinch a goal and the cup, at the same time I was screaming for anyone to score a goal even the bloody ref. It was starting to dawn on me that if it ended up a draw these buggers would be playing the replay on my pitch on Thursday. 'Score you B****'s score', but they couldn't have heard me as the game ended in one each, replay at Wembley Stadium on Thursday night, kick off 7.45. Tickets on sale Sunday morning, lovely I thought, bloody lovely.

As there were no winners that day, there wasn't the usual lap of honour by the teams, only a sort of half-hearted trot around to thank their fans and perhaps encourage them to come back on Thursday night. It was just as well that the celebrations weren't too prolonged on the pitch because now we needed to get on to it, repairing what we could while we could. It couldn't all wait until Sunday this time because Brazil was going to play England on Tuesday night and three days just wasn't enough time to prepare, not in these conditions and guess what, there was a flood-lit practice match scheduled for Sunday evening. Can you believe the Brazilian International Squad, needing to practice? Someone was having a laugh and it certainly wasn't me.

Black Sunday morning and it was pouring with rain, although it hadn't deterred the fans from turning up to get their tickets for the FA Cup replay. Some hadn't gone home at all, presumably Manchester supporters, they had just slept where they could and started lining up first thing. By the time I arrived, there were hundreds of cars trying to get into the stadium car parks, the roads were choked with traffic. I eventually got to the Palace of Arts where I have to sign in and pulled the car to the side of the road disgusted at being 45 minutes late and was about to leap out when I got the dulcet tones of a very large and dripping wet policeman. "Get that thing out of here" he said, pointing at my car. I in turn pointed at the special Wembley pass on the windscreen which didn't impress him one bit and he started reading me the riot act. I argued for a while but as I was getting nowhere jumped out of the car, dived into the offices, signed in, and jumped back again, not a simple manoeuvre for someone my size. The policeman went potty, if it hadn't been for the length of the traffic jam behind me he'd have booked me for sure, he didn't care if I was the Pope, never mind the Head Groundsman.

I continued to crawl along Engineers Way in the traffic dodging between the cars and fans eager to get tickets for the replay and eventually I got to the Pedway where I turned in. "Oi" shouted a smaller and possibly even wetter policeman, "You can't put that thing in here, back out". I wound the window down and very calmly told him that as I was the Head Groundsman there may not be a replay if I didn't get in. He burst out laughing and called to one of his pals nearby "Here's another one, we've had the Managing Director, the bloody referee, now we've got the groundsman".

I sat there fuming, of all the coppers I knew in and around Wembley I had to pick a comedian and all the time the cars behind were hooting and the policemen stayed in front of my car defiant. Just then a WPC, who'd been talking to me at the match the day before, came along and said to me "Good morning, not a nice day for your work, is it?" PC Comic realised she knew me and presumably deduced that I might just be who I said I was. He kind of sidled to one side and very half-heartedly, let me through but was almost run over by the convoy of cars behind me who now thought there was somewhere else to park. What a morning and I hadn't got in the ground yet.

Just as I expected, when I got down to the pitch I found it was badly cut up and no amount of repairing could alter the scars that defaced the sacred turf. It's not so bad when the divots can be put back where they came from, in time they knit into place. But where you have just a hole gouged out of the surface the answer is to fill it with the mixture of grass seeds, soils and fertilisers that will match the rest of the pitch. Unfortunately, that takes a little while to grow through and until it does, it looks exactly what it is, a hole filled with soil. There are those amongst us who assume that we can patch the offending marks with pieces of turf which although it is possible isn't ideal. The trouble with that is some superstar footballer is just as likely to kick one of these patches up in the air instead of the ball. That would be annoying to the player, hysterical to the crowd and downright embarrassing to me.

By the middle of Sunday afternoon, the ground staff had done all that could be done to put the pitch right, all it really needed was a little time to heal and a brief spell of dry weather. The weather and time were of course in the lap of the Gods but the Brazilians knock about that was due that very evening was down to mere mortals, so I went to the boss and asked that the practice match for that night be put off, I was told it couldn't be changed.

On another occasion, this life-long fan would have hung around to watch the greatest players in the world just kicking a ball around. But instead, I went home wet, weary and a bit disgusted. At long last that pitch had been made into one of the best drained playing surfaces to be found anywhere, but no pitch can take so much rain without showing it. Enclosed as it is the ground doesn't get the circulation of air that's necessary to dry out during prolonged rainy periods. The drains under the pitch, although ideal under most conditions, share the same drainage system with the rest of the stadium, its car parks and buildings. So, when the sewers back up as they did on this occasion the water from the pitch had nowhere to go. Which was just about where I felt that I had reached.

On arrival Monday morning I walked straight out onto the terraces to get a view of the pitch, it had been torn to ribbons again, it had really taken some punishment this time. On closer inspection much of the damage was in the goal areas and corners where a good deal of 'practice' had taken place for the set-pieces yet again. The divots that were replaced were so muddy it was difficult to see at a glance which way up they should be, and out of this we were supposed to produce a playing surface worthy of an International Match. Anyway, despite the blooming rain and despite my own opinion of the pitch, the Brazilians put on a wonderful display. The skills that those players showed that night made me think that there was still hope for football yet, they were brilliant, and I always thought they preferred a firm dry surface. Just goes to show, if you've got it, you've got it. So, someone remind me again, why did they need the practice?

I didn't get home until after midnight and tried to forget that we had to go in on Wednesday to make the pitch good enough for an FA Cup Final, the replay was on Thursday night and on the following Saturday there was yet another cup final, the FA Trophy but not to worry, that was four days away yet, I'd think about it nearer the time, maybe tomorrow.

Wednesday and Thursday came and went, we were starting to go through the motions of preparing the surface like zombies, but when the Manchester City and Tottenham supporters started to pour into the stadium they actually brought a breath of fresh air with them.

Their enthusiasm hadn't been subdued by the game on Saturday, if anything the banners seemed to be bigger and the singing louder and it even brought me back to life. Then, to everyone's astonishment the teams put on the show that had been promised on Saturday but not delivered, and at that moment I didn't care about the pitch or anything other than stopping to watch this fantastic game of football. Every-thing that a Cup Final ought to be, was in this game, the players really turned it on, and I who have become somewhat blasé about the actual performances, was as noisy as anyone there. Not for any one team either. I didn't care who won or lost, it was just an exciting game and a pleasure to be there and for once the final whistle came too soon, something you won't hear me say very often. For the record the Spurs won the cup that night, deservedly so in my view but I might be somewhat biased.

The euphoria went soon enough though, actually it went by the next morning as we stood on the wet wreck that had once been the sacred turf of Wembley and wondered where to start for the best. I think we must have tossed a coin or something but for two pins we'd have all gone home there and then. I say all, there wasn't that many of the ground staff anyway, but those that were there were pretty sick of repairing the repairs and seeing little to show for it. The blokes were working their socks off for hours and at the end of a day it was as though no-one had been there at all.

It wasn't doing me much good either, although I wasn't supposed to do physical work, under the circumstances I was doing just that, you can't help it, but it was beginning to tell a bit. For that matter it was beginning to tell on all of us, what with the pitch being used every other day or night every available person was working on the playing surface all of the time.

We had got the Trophy Final over with, and on Sunday just three of us went in to repair the pitch for what seemed like the hundredth time. It poured with rain all the time we were out there, and we only came off when the rain got too heavy to work in, and we were too weary to be bothered. It seemed a hopeless task, putting the ground to rights knowing that it wasn't the answer. The ground needed to dry out and be left for a fortnight, only then would we have something that we could work with. But that wasn't going to happen, with the Cup Finals over we could now look forward to the Home Internationals. On the coming Wednesday night England would be at home to Wales, but before that Wales would need a practice match, and that would take place on Tuesday, and that I was told was definite.

When the players arrived and had a look around, the Wales Team Manager, Mike England was very understanding and had the good sense to restrict his players to the areas that had taken the least punishment. Despite which, the next morning saw the old girl spewing up once again.

The match came and went and to me was of no particular consequence especially as there was going to be the big one on Saturday, England against Scotland and the Scottish squad would of course need to have a period of practice on the Wembley pitch the very next day. Terrific.

On Thursday they had their practice match, and on Saturday they had the real thing. They played to a television audience of millions plus the 100,000 in the stadium, it was a typical England - Scotland affair.

Me, I watched it all on the television at home because the conditions had finally caught up with me, and I was confined to bed with a raging cold or flu or both. It was just as well, I didn't really see or care about the game, all I could see was that wet pitch with more damaged than undamaged surface for those teams to play on and for the first time I was ashamed of the Wembley pitch that I claimed to be the best in the World.

In previous years the commentators and press have often made much of the pitch when it wasn't up to the mark, but funnily enough, this time when it really was in such a state it was barely mentioned. But I knew it was wrong and although the club grounds all over the country suffered far worse and looked it, the Wembley pitch could have been given a chance to live up to its reputation as the premier ground in the country and to allow players to perform to the best of their abilities. But it doesn't get every chance, nor every resource or consideration as some people believe and the significance of its green striped pitch as its focal point, not just the structure, seems somehow lost to the powers that be at that time.

It doesn't take a lot of imagination to realize that there is more to creating and maintaining an important playing surface than looking after the average garden lawn. Unfortunately, whether it's a stadium for football, rugby, cricket or tennis, to many of those responsible for and in control of these arenas, the pitch is simply another part of the building. An example of this ignorance occurred, on the wrong pitch at a time when it was important that it shouldn't have happened.

The day after the England, Scotland match and in the absence of myself and my deputy who was also ill at home, the men in grey suits took responsibility for repairing the pitch and although there was an assistant head groundsman on call, he wasn't the type to argue against officialdom when he was allocated three men who had never been on the pitch in their lives. He tried to muddle through. On that Sunday there were men available from the heavy gang who had worked with turf for years and knew exactly what was needed. But they weren't called upon, instead a manager went to the canteen and asked for volunteers to work on the pitch, that's how much thought went into maintaining the most famous turf in the world.

I didn't know about this until I returned to work a few days later and although the usual ground staff had seen the results already, they had chosen to leave the pitch exactly as they had found it, partly in disgust, partly because they knew that I would want to see it for myself.

Whether done in haste or ignorance didn't matter, the pitch was an absolute mess with holes partially filled with soil but no seed, with strips of turf partially folded under, the grass dying and muddy divots actually pressed into the ground upside down. The old joke about the foreman instructing the workmen how to lay turf pointing out that it was 'green side up' didn't strike me as funny because someone should have told these blokes that's what they had to do.

It wasn't the fault of the men, they should never have been asked to do a job they knew nothing about. It wasn't really the fault of the assistant head groundsman, not many people can stand up to authority and he couldn't have overseen everyone all over the pitch. But it was the fault of the gentleman who appears to have obtained management skills from a d.i.y manual and knowledge of grass from a 50p gardening magazine. Second thoughts, he couldn't have, gardeners knew that you lay turf 'green side up'.

Needless to say, a confrontation occurred, and I made sure that I had the General Manager among the audience. I spelled out the cost in man hours of putting right what had been done wrong knowing that whatever other considerations prevailed, cost is the language that they understand. But I used the gardening magazine analogy as well, the rest I leave to your imagination. I did the unthinkable by suggesting that in future they keep off my pitch for as long as it was my pitch. So far so good.

Apart from another schoolboy international match two weeks later my busy period was almost done. There wouldn't be another big game until the Charity Shield match in August, although there would be the fabulous Military Pageant.

Between times the pitch would get a real dose of medicine from me and my crew, even though the events peter out in the summer, the disease and problems go on and the time without matches to worry about would be well spent restoring the pitch to the conditions that I wanted it to be in. As long as I would be allowed to have the final say in the matter, however small that 'say' is, the sacred turf of Wembley would be made to live up to its reputation because what the powers that be hadn't considered was, that it was my reputation too.

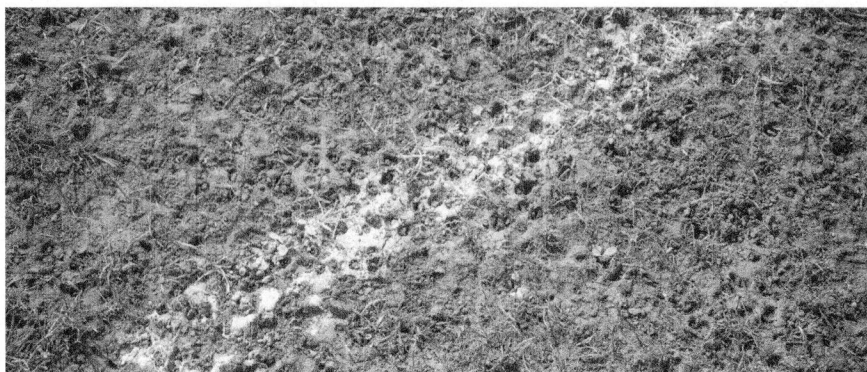

© Lance Bellers | Dreamstime.com

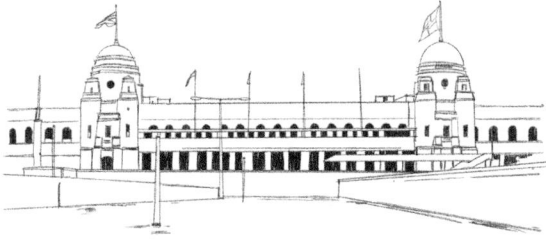

©NikkiHazelton

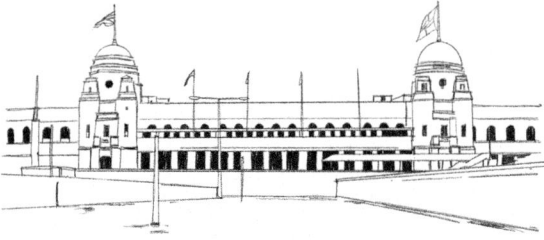

Chapter 14

The Final

On the 5th of October 1985, my 65th birthday plus one day old, I was retired as Head Groundsman of the most famous stadium in the world. Note the expression that I 'was retired', it wasn't my idea, I didn't retire, who would have, given a choice? I never claimed that Wembley Stadium was the best, but it is among the most famous and certainly most talked about sports grounds on the 'I wannabee the groundsman' list of groundsmen. To say I was a reluctant retiree would be about the biggest understatement of my life, as I believed I was at my peak in terms of knowledge, particularly about Wembley, its pitch and the variety of demands expected of it. But those were the rules, and it was 65 and goodbye. Who dreamt that one up? I for one was definitely not ready to go, I was after all a late starter and a decade was not nearly enough at this place, I felt that I had so much more to do and a lot more I wanted to give. During the last few years in particular, I seemed to be meeting or talking to people on the phone from Newcastle to Argentina, from the Middle East to the USA, seeking advice and sharing experiences. Typically, from superintendents of stadia of every size and purpose and in one case a poor devil, just a few weeks away from a major event with a playing surface more suited to a gymkhana, going by the photos in the newspaper, than a World Cup showpiece. Not for the first time a host country had built an impressive stadium and 'by the way' laid some turf in the middle, for 'them' to play on.

When will the architects and engineers ask for input from someone who might know if the centrepiece playing surface might be affected by airflow or lack of it, drainage or lack of it and if laying turf as though laying a carpet was going to work. Then, get it down a bit longer than a few weeks before it was to be used and give it the fullest attention to make sure that it stays down and allowed to knit and to grow.

With so many good examples of world class pitches to be found around the world why do they re-invent the wheel so many times? Is it really because the groundsman is still regarded as an afterthought in a cloth cap who cuts the grass and marks lines out? Do they still believe that it's only a step up from just another lawn, so that all that is needed is some very expensive consultants on turf management, organisations with oodles of research in grasses which suit every purpose. Except perhaps, that 'every' purpose doesn't always equate to the same variety of grass being 'used' week in week out, in less than 'laboratory' conditions.

And with newspaper back page headlines of a stadium and especially the pitch not being ready in time for a major event, a few of my global colleagues became the centre of media storms, sending out cries of help to salvage a situation that they hadn't been party to until the damage was done.

It is an international disgrace, it is ....! Well, you know from what I have put in these pages what they would have said to me and how they would be paying personally just to keep a job, I wasn't likely to miss any of that in retirement.

Sorry, for going off on one again, but that was at the heart of so many conversations with my counterparts around the country and around the world. But for 'a Ha'porth of tar' the ship was lost etc; But for putting the playing surface on the list of considerations when building a stadium. But for paying ground staff overtime to water the pitch during a drought the 'sacred turf' was lost (the Wembley 'number crunchers' did that more than once). In my early career at amateur sport level, a small club I was associated with spent over £30,000 re-fitting the bar and facilities but could find nothing in the budget for grass seed or groundsman's wages. Repeatedly the treasurer found it out of his own pocket but only after my going to him literally 'cap in hand'. The fact was that we had now got the Wembley pitch about right, something to be proud of that so many visitors called or came to see what we had achieved and wanted to know how to emulate that. Players played good football and despite extra time, were not rolling around in agony caused by cramp. Bring on as many events as you want, cover the turf with wooden panels and tarpaulin for a concert, we will cope and so will the turf. Giving up at that point wasn't a good feeling.

I was at least continuing the tradition of leaving my successor with the best ground staff I had ever had the pleasure to work with. Headed up by Jim Hawes, Alan Malzard, Gerry Smith and Reg Barwick. The young man who took my place as Head Groundsman, Steve Tingley, is in my opinion one of the best men at the craft of Turf culture in Britain today and only in his mid-twenties so believe it or not I was as proud as I was reluctant when he took over the reins from me.

I was also to remain on the books as a consultant for another twelve months and thereafter on a somewhat ad hoc arrangement. Ad hoc inasmuch as we agreed terms which became 'don't call us we will call you' when we need help. It wasn't Steve, he knew I was on the end of a phone and could call for advice anytime and he kept me in touch for a long time to come. Good friends such as the Groundsman's Institute and others helped by being a conduit for those that wanted to tap into this old head full of knowledge from around the country and occasionally from further afield.

But all that would come later, on the final day as Head Groundsman, I shook hands and said my goodbyes with everyone, some of the lads came in on their day off just to make sure I was going, some said. As I walked out of the offices and drove away from the stadium, I couldn't come to terms with the reality that although it wasn't for the last time, the pitch was no longer to be my responsibility, not my concern, not my baby. But the baby had at least reached maturity and I was definitely leaving it in a far better condition than I had found it but that was precious little consolation.

I feel that having put much of my experiences to paper I should at this point conclude with a poignant exit line, something about walking away from the stadium along Olympic Way and turning back to look over my shoulder at the famous Twin Towers for the last time as Head Groundsman.

But unlike my dramatic entrance a decade or so previously, I was in the car, dealing with my own thoughts and it didn't occur to me to do something so symbolic. If I'd have known I was going to write a book, I should have had someone take a picture.

Don Gallacher
Head Groundsman
Empire Stadium, Wembley

1974 – 1985

Don Gallacher 1919–1997

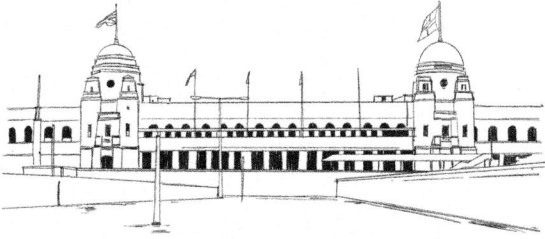

Added Time

Don was employed as a consultant to Wembley for another twelve months or so and even though after a lifetime in North London, he and the family moved house from Tottenham to Northamptonshire. Wembley Stadium management were seemingly happy to cover the cost of additional travel to get him back to the pitch when needed. Although going by some correspondence to his brother Terry, the relationship seemed to run hot and cold.

In a letter to his youngest brother Terry, 25th August 1986

.... *'I still go down to Wembley now and again ..... there was a problem at first with tax and mileage cost from Wellingborough, but the top boss at the stadium said 'I want Don and I want him now. Work something out.' they worked something out, so I am happy and Wembley appear to be satisfied'.*

Don also acted as a consultant for others for some time, responding to occasional requests for help with sports grounds large and small, he said that he enjoyed going back to the cricket grounds in particular, I believe that was his first love, certainly as a player. But he wasn't offered a job at Lords, although he was offered the job at Melbourne Cricket Club many years previously, but that is yet another story.

He told me that he didn't get as much consultancy work, to keep him as busy as he would have liked. But it took him a while to realise that one problem was an assumption on the part of potential enquirers, that the former Head Groundsman, Wembley Stadium, was above their budget and it didn't occur to them to ask. Little did they know that the prestigious title never did relate to his salary even when he was at the top of his game, the rewards were not good by any standard.

But there were high points too, as suggested in another letter to his brother Terry, which I came across only recently and knew nothing about the occasion. It falls somewhere between his unfailing optimistic search for a new career path and 'a grand day out'.

In a letter to his brother Terry 9th April 1987

Dear Terry

............I have all the time in the world now, the only thing I do is type, I do a lot of articles for Trade Magazines, not all are printed in full but it means a few bob now and again, as well as corresponding with people who simply ask me things or say hello.

I was at Wembley on Sunday for the Littlewoods Cup Final in the strange position of supporting a commentator for BBC Radio (Northampton), I wasn't paid but I had a really good time, met all the lads as well as a few VIPS and for once I didn't feel as though I should stay in the background.

It came about from a suggestion by the local BBC who had done an item on my moving to Northamptonshire. They would cover the Cup Final and have me as their own expert to talk about the Wembley pitch, which I readily agreed to. They sent a car to pick me up at nine in the morning and we started talking on the recording machine as soon as we left my front gate. You know the thing 'Well Don, here we are leaving your home for the seventy odd miles to Wembley and some six hours before the kick-off, how does it feel?' and all that sort of thing. We also talked as we went down the motorway and when we arrived at the stadium entrance among the crowds of fans, I realised that all he had to get in was a letter from the Public Relations Manager and from previous experience I told him he would never get into the stadium without a day pass. Well, the letter inviting all the BBC personnel, plus me not only got us past all the jobs-worth's but we were afforded the best treatment. I have previously told you that I believed that I had been forgotten. Far from it, I wasn't just a name on a list, I was mentioned in the Wembley letter with affection, being referred to as 'Our Don'.

The pitch was fantastic. Steve Tingley (present head groundsman) met us in the middle of the pitch with a big grin on his face as well as the three lads who had been part of my staff. It was wonderful, and quite emotional. We went to lunch and had a couple of pints, something I hadn't done for twelve months. Then into the seats provided by the Football League, £25.00 each and right next to the Royal Box and the most comfortable I had ever sat in. After the match we went back down onto the pitch and carried on interviewing ground staff. It seemed that this was a new approach to commenting on a big match, having the inside track as it were through my knowledge. The part I liked most was answering questions while watching the game. People sitting around us must have thought we were mad talking to ourselves; they could not have seen the mikes. An edited recording of it went out at 1.30pm on Sunday and some of it was live from the match but I don't know which part. It could lead to further work. Phil Malone who was the BBC chap with me seems to think it will, it is funny I am always being told this but it never happens, sometimes it's my own fault. I was on nine different TV stations *when the American Football was first here and all made offers, Betty will not travel and I will not go without her. She is nervous enough when I go to Preston or Macclesfield for one night, she will not stay in the house alone, not without arranging the divorce first. I had a great many offers from different firms when it was announced that I was retiring, I chose the offer from Wembley and in 1985 that was three times a week, but it also meant turning down all the other people who wanted me as a consultant. I fell between two stools as usual......*

Don continued to enjoy ill health for a number of years, claiming at one point to have been a patient in every ward of Kettering Hospital except Maternity, and he was working on that.

In a letter to his brother Terry, 5th November 1995

'I am perfectly aware that I am not the only one who has illness, what annoys me is the fact that we were all so bloody fit for most of our lives. Every time I have a doctor in he finds something else wrong, I told the latest doctor that he reminded me of a cowboy builder who makes a point to look for something else wrong so as to keep him in work'.

'By the way, my other hobby is writing poetry, not the 'pretty-pretty' stuff, I have written about thirty poems so far and one has been accepted by a publisher, I call it 'The Cry of a Bosnian Child', I will send you a copy.

.... All My Love'

Don

It wasn't just poetry that kept him occupied. I can remember as small children our dad telling us bedtime stories of knights of old and dragons and fanciful things that came straight out of his head. He clearly had a wonderful imagination and I understand that he did the same with his next generation family of children and grandchildren. A regular creation was stories about characters that lived in an 'Old English Village' with colourful names and likely a voice to match each individual. Even I recognise some of the people, places and tales that came from real life, especially those of them attending a cricket match on the local village green.

When we were children, my brother Don, my sister Pat and I, along with aunts, uncles and cousins went to those village green cricket matches. So I know that they weren't all fanciful imagination, but tales taken from real-life.

As is of course, every 'story' in this book.

Gallacher Family days out - cricket on village greens

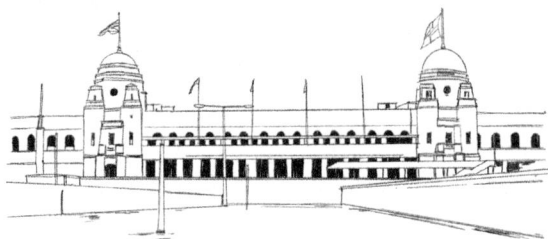

Acknowledgements

Over such a long period of time it will be no surprise that a number of people have given their time, impartial advice and expertise in helping me to bring Dad's work to fruition. Including most recently, Don Gallacher Junior, Ian Gallacher, Justin Gallacher, Linda Gallacher, Nikki Hazelton (nee Gallacher) and Yvonne Gallacher. But I must include a former colleague Lynn Davies, who from the very beginning, as with others, sat with Dad in my office, typing up his hand-written pages, typed as in with a typewriter. He later typed his own and the manuscript went through a dozen iterations of technology since then. Thanks Lynn and thank you all.

Book cover design: Ian Gallacher

Book photo design: Ian Gallacher

Drawings by: radennorfiqri

Picture Acknowledgements

The author and publisher would like to thank the following copyright holders for permission and licence to reproduce images in this book including:

Alamy Stock Photo

CGfamily Photos

Dreamstime

Gallacher Family Archives

Historic England. (HES)

Merv Payne, Victor Publishing

Nikki Hazelton Photography

PA/PA Archive/PA Images

Reach Publishing Services/Mirrorpix

The Francis Frith Collection

The Hockey Museum

Orphan Photographs.

The author and publisher have made all reasonable efforts to contact copyright holders for permission and apologise for any omissions or errors in the form of credits given. We continue with that search and subject to further contact, corrections will be made to future publications.

Meanwhile our thanks to the organisations and platforms for their assistance and guidance into locating the copyright holders.

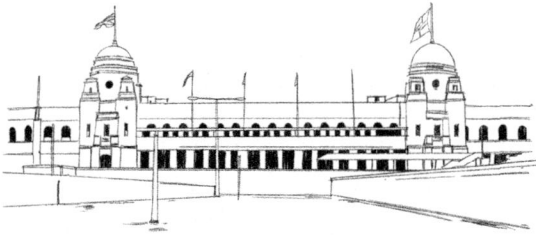

The original Wembley Stadium, (known as the Empire Stadium) was a football stadium in Wembley, London, best known for hosting important football matches. It stood on the same site now occupied by its (New) successor.

Now in its centenary year, Wembley hosted the FA Cup final annually, the first in 1923, which was the stadium's inaugural event, the League Cup final annually, five European Cup finals, the 1966 World Cup final, and the final of Euro 1996.

The stadium also hosted many other sports events, including the 1948 Summer Olympics, rugby league's Challenge Cup final, the 1992 and 1995 Rugby League World Cup finals and the World Speedway Championships. It was also the venue for numerous music events, including the 1985 Live Aid charity concert. Mainly due to it being one of the few stadia in its day, to accommodate up to 100,000 spectators and frequently did.

The following pages provide an example of the number of events that took place at the original Wembley Stadium during the period (1974-1985) when Don Gallacher was the Head Groundsman, curator of the 'sacred turf'.

FA Cup finals   1975–1985

The Football Association Challenge Cup, commonly known as the FA Cup, is a knockout competition in English football, organised by and named after The Football Association (The FA).   The vast majority of FA Cup Final matches have been in London: most of these were played at the original Wembley Stadium, from 1923 until the stadium closed in 2000.

Year	Team	Result	Team	Venue	Attendance
May 75	West Ham	2-0	Fulham	Wembley Stadium	100,000
May 76	Southampton	1-0	Manchester United	Wembley Stadium	99.115
May 77	Manchester Utd	2-1	Liverpool	Wembley Stadium	99,252
May 78	Ipswich Town	1-0	Arsenal	Wembley Stadium	100,000
May 79	Arsenal	1-0	Manchester United	Wembley Stadium	99,219
May 80	West Ham	1-0	Arsenal	Wembley Stadium	100,000
May 81	Tottenham Hotspur	1-1	Manchester City	Wembley Stadium	100,000
		2-3 (R)			92,000
May 82	Tottenham Hotspur	1-1	Queens Park Rangers	Wembley Stadium	100,000
		1-0 (R)			100,000
May 83	Manchester Utd	2-2	Brighton & Hove Albion	Wembley Stadium	100,000
		0-4 (R)			91,534
May 84	Everton	2-0	Watford	Wembley Stadium	100,000
May 85	Everton	0-1	Manchester United	Wembley Stadium	100,000

EFL Cup finals 1975–1985

The EFL Cup is a knockout cup competition in English football organised by and named after the English Football League (EFL). The competition was established in 1960 and is considered to be the second-most important domestic cup competition for English football clubs, after the FA Cup.

Year	Team	Result	Team	Venue	Attendance
Mar 75	Aston Villa	1–0	Norwich City	Wembley Stadium	95,946
Feb 76	Manchester City	2–1	Newcastle United	Wembley Stadium	100,000
Mar 77	Aston Villa	0–0	Everton	Wembley Stadium	100,000
Mar 78	Nottingham Forest	0–0	Liverpool	Wembley Stadium	100,000
Mar 79	Nottingham Forest	3–2	Southampton	Wembley Stadium	96,952
Mar 80	Wolverhampton Wanderers	1–0	Nottingham Forest	Wembley Stadium	96,527
Mar 81	Liverpool	1–1	West Ham United	Wembley Stadium	100,000
Mar 82	Liverpool	3–1	Tottenham Hotspur	Wembley Stadium	100,000
Mar 83	Liverpool	2–1	Manchester United	Wembley Stadium	99,304
Mar 84	Liverpool	0–0	Everton	Wembley Stadium	100,000
Mar 85	Norwich City	1–0	Sunderland	Wembley Stadium	100,000

International Football at Wembley: 1975-1985

England played its first game at Wembley's Empire Stadium in 1924. Just 10 home games were played outside of the Empire Stadium in the period 1951 until 1999. In1984: The Home Championships came to an end, announcing that the 1983–84 British Home Championship would be their last.

Home					
Year	Team	Result	Team	Venue	Attendance
May 75	England	2-2	Wales	Wembley Stadium	53.000
May 75	England	5-1	Scotland	Wembley Stadium	98,241
May 76	England	4-0	Northern Ireland	Wembley Stadium	48,000
May 77	England	0-1	Wales	Wembley Stadium	48,000
Jun 77	England	0-2	Scotland	Wembley Stadium	98,103
May 78	England	1-0	Northern Ireland	Wembley Stadium	48,000
May 79	England	0-0	Wales	Wembley Stadium	70,220
May 79	England	3-1	Scotland	Wembley Stadium	100,000
May 80	England	1-1	Northern Ireland	Wembley stadium	33,676
May 81	England	0-0	Wales	Wembley Stadium	34,280
May 81	England	0-1	Scotland	Wembley Stadium	90,000
Feb 82	England	4-0	Northern Ireland	Wembley Stadium	54,900
Feb 83	England	2-1	Wales	Wembley Stadium	24,000
June 83	England	2-0	Scotland	Wembley Stadium	83,000
April 84	England	1-0	Northern Ireland	Wembley Stadium	24,000

International Friendly					
Year	Team	Result	Team	Venue	Attendance
Mar 75	England	2-0	West Germany	Wembley Stadium	98,000
Sep 76	England	1-1	Rep of Ireland	Wembley Stadium	51,000
Sep 77	England	0-0	Switzerland	Wembley Stadium	42,000
Apr 78	England	1-1	Brazil	Wembley Stadium	92,500
May 78	England	4-1	Hungary	Wembley Stadium	74,000
Nov 78	England	1-0	Czechoslovakia	Wembley Stadium	92,000
May 80	England	3-1	Argentina	Wembley Stadium	90,000
Mar 81	England	1-2	Spain	Wembley Stadium	71,840
May 81	England	0-1	Brazil	Wembley Stadium	75,000
May 82	England	2-0	The Netherlands	Wembley Stadium	68,000
Oct 82	England	1-2	West Germany	Wembley Stadium	67,500
Jun 84	England	0-2	USSR	Wembley Stadium	38,125
Sep 84	England	1-0	East Germany	Wembley Stadium	23,951
Mar 85	England	2-1	Republic of Ireland	Wembley Stadium	34,793

World Cup Qualifier					
Year	Team	Result	Team	Venue	Attendance
Oct 76	England	2-1	Finland	Wembley Stadium	87,000
Mar 77	England	5-0	Luxembourg	Wembley Stadium	81,718
Nov 77	England	2-0	Italy	Wembley Stadium	92,000
Sep 80	England	4-0	Norway	Wembley Stadium	48,250
Nov 80	England	2-1	Switzerland	Wembley Stadium	69,000
Apr 81	England	0-0	Romania	Wembley Stadium	62,500
Nov 81	England	1-0	Hungary	Wembley Stadium	92,000
Oct 84	England	5-0	Finland	Wembley Stadium	47,234
Sep 85	England	1-1	Romania	Wembley Stadium	59,500
Oct 85	England	5-0	Turkey	Wembley Stadium	52,500

European Championship Qualifier					
Year	Team	Result	Team	Venue	Attendance
Oct 74	England	3-0	Czechoslovakia	Wembley Stadium	83,858
Nov 74	England	0-0	Portugal	Wembley Stadium	84,461
Apr 75	England	5-0	Cyprus	Wembley Stadium	68,245
Feb 79	England	4-0	Northern Ireland	Wembley Stadium	92,000
Sep 79	England	1-0	Denmark	Wembley Stadium	82,000
Nov 79	England	2-0	Bulgaria	Wembley Stadium	71,491
Dec 82	England	9-0	Luxembourg	Wembley Stadium	33,980
Mar 83	England	0-0	Greece	Wembley Stadium	44,051
Apr 83	England	2-0	Hungary	Wembley Stadium	54,000
Sep 83	England	0-1	Denmark	Wembley Stadium	82,500
European Cup Final					
May 78	Liverpool	1-0	FC Bruges	Wembley Stadium	92,000

The Women's Hockey Internationals

In 1951, the All England Women's Hockey Association (AEWHA) arranged the first of its 41 London Internationals to be played at the old Wembley Stadium. The programme for the day proudly announced that this was the first time that a women's team game had been played at the famous Empire Stadium. The only gap in this amazing record was 1970 when the condition of the Wembley pitch resulted in the match being transferred at short notice to The White City Stadium.

Date	Team	Result	Opposition	Venue	Attendance
Mar 75	England	2-0	Wales	Wembley Stadium	65,000
Mar 76	England	3-0	Scotland	Wembley Stadium	68,000
Mar 77	England	1-0	New Zealand	Wembley Stadium	65,000
Mar 78	England	2-2	USA	Wembley Stadium	66,000
Mar 79	England	0-0	Ireland	Wembley Stadium	66,000
Mar 80	England	2-0	Scotland	Wembley Stadium	65,000
Mar 81	England	2-1	Wales	Wembley Stadium	62,000
Mar 82	England	2-4	Netherlands	Wembley Stadium	62,000
Mar 83	England	3-2	F R Germany	Wembley Stadium	55,000
Mar 84	England	0-1	Ireland	Wembley Stadium	47,000
Mar 85	England	3-0	Scotland	Wembley Stadium	41,000

The FA Charity Shield (Community Shield)

The Football Association Community Shield (formerly the Charity Shield) is an annual association football match organised by the Football Association and presently contested between the champions of the Premier League and the winners of the FA Cup. Since 1974, all but seven of the matches have been held at either the original or new Wembley stadiums.

Year	Team	Result	Team	Venue	Attendance
Aug 75	Derby County	2–0	West Ham United	Wembley Stadium	59,000
Aug 76	Liverpool	1–0	Southampton	Wembley Stadium	76,500
Aug 77	Liverpool	0–0	Manchester United	Wembley Stadium	82,000
Aug 78	Nottingham Forest	5–0	Ipswich Town	Wembley Stadium	68,000
Aug 79	Liverpool	3–1	Arsenal	Wembley Stadium	92,800
Aug 80	Liverpool	1–0	West Ham United	Wembley Stadium	90,000
Aug 81	Aston Villa	2–2	Tottenham Hotspur	Wembley Stadium	92,500
Aug 82	Liverpool	1–0	Tottenham Hotspur	Wembley Stadium	82,500
Aug 83	Manchester United	2–0	Liverpool	Wembley Stadium	92,000
Aug 84	Everton	1–0	Liverpool	Wembley Stadium	100,000
Aug 85	Everton	2–0	Manchester United	Wembley Stadium	82,000

The FA Vase

The Football Association Challenge Vase, commonly known as the FA Vase, is a knockout cup competition in English football, organised by and named after The Football Association (the FA). It was staged for the first time in the 1974–75 season, effectively replacing the FA Amateur Cup, which was discontinued after the abolition of official amateur status by the FA.

Year	Team	Result	Team	Venue
Apr 75	Hoddeson Town	2–1	Epsom & Ewell	Wembley Stadium
Apr 76	Billericay Town	1–0	Stamford	Wembley Stadium
Apr 77	Billericay Town	1–1	Sheffield	Wembley Stadium
Apr 78	Blue Star	2–1	Barton Rovers	Wembley Stadium
Apr 79	Billericay Town	4–1	Almondsbury Greenway	Wembley Stadium
Apr 80	Stamford	2–0	Guisborough Town	Wembley Stadium
Apr 81	Whickham	3–2	Willenhall Town	Wembley Stadium
Apr 82	Forest Green Rovers	3–0	Rainworth Miners Welfare	Wembley Stadium
Apr 83	VS Rugby	1–0	Halesowen Town	Wembley Stadium
Apr 84	Stansted	3–2	Stamford	Wembley Stadium
Apr 85	Halesowen Town	3–1	Fleetwood Town	Wembley Stadium

Schoolboy International (English Schools Football Association)

Year	Team	Result	Team	Venue	Attendance
Mar 75	England	4-0	The Netherlands	Wembley Stadium	40,000
Jun 75	England	0-1	Scotland	Wembley Stadium	not known
Mar 76	England	4-1	Wales	Wembley Stadium	not known
Jun 76	England	6-1	France	Wembley Stadium	not known
Mar 77	England	2-0	Scotland	Wembley Stadium	not known
Jun 77	England	1-2	West Germany	Wembley Stadium	not known
Mar 78	England	3-3	France	Wembley Stadium	not known
May 78	England	3-0	Scotland	Wembley Stadium	61,000
Mar 79	England	1-1	Wales	Wembley Stadium	not known
Jun 79	England	2-2	West Germany	Wembley Stadium	not known
Mar 80	England	2-0	Switzerland	Wembley Stadium	not known
Jun 80	England	4-5	Scotland	Wembley Stadium	69,000
Mar 81	England	4-0	Northern Ireland	Wembley Stadium	not known
Jun 81	England	1-2	West Germany	Wembley Stadium	not known
Mar 82	England	7-0	The Netherlands	Wembley Stadium	44,000
Jun 82	England	0-0	Scotland	Wembley Stadium	61,000

Schoolboy International (English Schools Football Association)

cont:

Year	Team	Result	Team	Venue	Attendance
Mar 83	England	1–0	West Germany	Wembley Stadium	not known
Jun 83	England	3–3	Scotland	Wembley Stadium	46,000
Mar 84	England	1–0	Scotland	Wembley Stadium	40,000
Jun 84	England	4–1	The Netherlands	Wembley Stadium	35,000
Mar 85	England	0–1	West Germany	Wembley Stadium	35,761
Jun 85	England	2–0	Switzerland	Wembley Stadium	31,653

The Inter–Varsity Soccer Match

Year	Team	Result	Team	Venue
Dec 74	Cambridge	1–3	Oxford	Wembley Stadium
Dec 75	Cambridge	0–2	Oxford	Wembley Stadium
Dec 76	Cambridge	0–0	Oxford	Wembley Stadium
Dec 77	Oxford	0–4	Cambridge	Wembley Stadium
Dec 78	Cambridge	2–1	Oxford	Wembley Stadium
Dec 79	Oxford	1–3	Cambridge	Wembley Stadium
Dec 80	Cambridge	0–2	Oxford	Wembley Stadium
Dec 81	Cambridge	0–2	Oxford	Wembley Stadium
Dec 82	Cambridge	2–4	Oxford	Wembley Stadium
Dec 83	Cambridge	2–2	Oxford	Wembley Stadium
Dec 84	Cambridge	4–2	Oxford	Wembley Stadium
Dec 85	Cambridge	2–0	Oxford	Wembley Stadium

The Challenge Cup of Rugby league 1974-1986

The Challenge Cup of Rugby League was instituted in the 1896–97. The final was played at many neutral venues up to and including 1928 after which it was mostly played at Wembley Stadium until 1939 just prior to the Second World War, 1941–45 after which it returned to Wembley in 1946 when the final permanently became a 'Wembley Final'.

Final	Team	Result	Team	Venue	Attendance
May 75	Widnes	14 – 7	Warrington	Wembley Stadium	85,098
May 76	St Helens	20 – 5	Widnes	Wembley Stadium	89,982
May 77	Leeds	16 – 7	Widnes	Wembley Stadium	80,871
May 78	Leeds	14 – 12	St Helens	Wembley Stadium	96,000
May 79	Widnes	12 - 3	Wakefield Trinity	Wembley Stadium	94,218
May 80	Hull Kingston Rovers	10 – 5	Hull FC	Wembley Stadium	95,000
May 81	Widnes	18 – 9	Hull Kingston Rovers	Wembley Stadium	92,496
May 82	Hull FC	14 – 14	Widnes	Wembley Stadium	92,147
May 83	Featherstone Rovers	14 – 12	Hull FC	Wembley Stadium	84,969
May 84	Widnes	19 – 6	Wigan	Wembley Stadium	80,116
May 85	Wigan	28 – 24	Hull FC	Wembley Stadium	97,801

Concerts held at Wembley Stadium include:

Date	Artist, Group, Event	Year	Concerts
		1974	1
Sep 14	Crosby, Stills, Nash and Young Joni Mitchell with Tom Scott and the L.A Express - The Band Jesse Colin Young.		80,000
		1975	1
Jun 21	Elton John – The Beach Boys – The Eagles Joe Walsh – Rufus featuring Chaka Khan Stackridge		72,000
		1979	1
Aug 18	The Who – The Stranglers – AC/DC Nils Lofgren		80,000
		1982	3
Jun 19	Simon & Garfunkel		72,000
Jul 25	The Rolling Stones – The J. Geils Band black uhuru		
Jul 26	The Rolling Stones – The J. Geils Band black uhuru		
		1984	2
Jun 30	The Summer of '84 Concert Elton John – Big Country Kool & The Gang – Nik Kershaw wang chung – Paul Young		
Jul 07	Bob Dylan – Santana - UB40		

Concerts held at Wembley Stadium include:

Cont:

Date	Artist, Group, Event	Year	Concerts
		1985	3
Jul 03	Bruce Springsteen		
Jul 04	Bruce Springsteen		
Jul 13	Live Aid Status Quo – The Style Council The Boomtown Rats – Adam Ant – Ultravox Spandau Ballet – Elvis Costello – Nik Kershaw Sade – Sting – Phil Collins – Branford Marsalis Howard Jones/ – Brian Ferry – Paul Young U2 – Dire Straits – Queen – David Bowie The Who – Elton John – Paul McCartney Band Aid.		

The Individual Speedway World Championship Final

The World Championship of Speedway is an international competition between the highest-ranked motorcycle speedway riders of the world, run under the auspices of the Fédération Internationale de Motocyclisme (FIM). The first official championships were held in 1936

Speedway Grand Prix are a series of stand-alone motorcycle speedway over the course of a season used to determine the Speedway World Champion.

Final	Winners	Runners Up	Third Place	Venue	Attendance
Sep 75	Ole Olsen	Anders Michanek	John Louis	Wembley Stadium	81,000
Sep 78	Ole Olsen	Gordon Kennett	Scott Autrey	Wembley Stadium	86,500
Sep 81	Bruce Penhall	Ole Olsen	Tommy Knudsen	Wembley Stadium	92,500

Note:

The 1981 Individual Speedway World Championship was the 36th edition of the official World Championship to determine the world champion rider.

It was also the last of a record 26 times that London's world famous Wembley Stadium hosted the World Final. It also marked the final time that the stadium would be used for any Motorcycle speedway. In future years when the final was held in England, it would be held at the Odsal Stadium in Bradford until the advent of the Speedway Grand Prix series in 1995. The 1981 Final was held before a reported crowd of 92,500, just shy of the Wembley record of 95,000 set at the 1938 World Final.

Individual events held at the original Wembley Stadium include:

Year	Event	Venue	Attendance
May 75	Evel Knievel	Wembley Stadium	60,000
On the 26 May 1975, in front of 60,000 pe ople, Evel Knievel, an American stunt performer and entertainer, crashed while trying to land a jump over 13 single decker city buses, an accident which resulted in his initial retirement from his daredevil life.			
May 82	The Papal Visit	Wembley Stadium	80,000
In the summer of 1982, Pope Saint John Paul II travelled to Great Britain for an historic six-day tour that saw him greet and bless hundreds of thousands of people at sixteen different venues. Wembley Stadium provided the setting for the first open-air Mass of Pope John Paul II's visit to Britain.			
Aug 83	American Football in London	Wembley Stadium	32,847
On the 6th August 1983 an NFL pre-season exhibition game between The Minnesota Vikings and The St Louis Cardinals. The Minnesota Vikings won 28-10. It was only the second time that American Football had been played at Wembley, the first being in 1952 when the stadium was host to the U.S. Airforce in Europe football championships, with the Fuerstenfeldbruck Eagles beating the Burtonwood Bullets 27-6.			
1978 1985	Wembley Stadium Tours	Wembley Stadium	Est in excess of 1,000,000

Statement

The information contained in the appendices of this book is for general information purposes only. The information is provided by various sources and while we endeavour to keep the information up to date and correct, we make no representations or warranties of any kind, express or implied, about the completeness, accuracy, reliability, suitability or availability with respect to the website or the information, products, services, or related graphics contained on the website for any purpose. Any reliance you place on such information is therefore strictly at your own risk.

Finally

And bearing in mind that the contents of these pages were written more than Forty years ago, I find it astonishing that so much of what my Dad experienced throughout his life as a groundsman, good, bad and really bad. Still remains true in many cases today, as I am discovering from ground persons who've shared their stories with me since publishing this book.

Particularly unfortunate that even the 'New' Wembley Stadium in its early years, made headlines for all the wrong reasons. Not least of which having to 'replace' the pitch 11 times. Fabulous stadium, but with top managers and players headline comments including: 'The pitch is a disgrace' and "it was not good enough for a Wembley pitch'. Whilst on at least one occasion, the groundsman shouldered the blame with his job.

Typical of the excuses given by management at the time included - 'In addition to showpiece football matches and rugby union club games, Wembley also stages rugby league's Challenge Cup final, NFL games, music concerts and has even hosted motorsport events in the past - around a dozen non-football events a year, in fact.'   Really?

How about this one: "We appreciate we have to improve the quality of the pitch and we are determined to do so," added the statement from Wembley's organisers.

Cant begin to imagine what my old man, or even my grandfather, would have said about this. Actually, I can, I've just helped write their story.

Colin Gallacher

The first Cup Final at Wembley Stadium, London, 1923,
Illustration from Wonderful London, Volume I,
published by Amalgamated Press, London

The demolition of the original Wembley Stadium,
begins in London c2002. In what was being seen as
the beginning of the end for the old Twin Towers,

Printed in Great Britain
by Amazon